## Advance Praise for

*All In: Community Engaged Scholarship for Social Change*

We have to thank Ana Antunes and Joy Howard for curating and editing *All In* - an inter-generational volume of essays crafted by progressive academics and organizers, from disparate fields including labor struggles, early childhood education, anti-racist schooling campaigns, food sovereignty and indigenous research practices. This volume is essential reading BEFORE you celebrate that your university has branded itself dedicated to "community-centered research." When activist scholarship becomes normative, it's time to worry - and check in with these writers who are deliciously and with complexity committed to deep epistemic justice, democratic participation, decolonizing practices and research for and with movements for justice. These chapters span the intimate and the global. They are borne in universities, in community-based movement spaces, across transnational borders and in yeasty conversations held in labor halls/bodegas/coffee shops/CBOs/child care centers and even philanthropies where freedom dreams are borne for just research tithed always to action. These are not "projects" but windows into lifetime commitments to building worlds not yet, engaged by those most impacted by social injustice, collaborating with those who are organizing, those who are researching, those who are trying to imagine life with purpose. Each chapter sketches a story about how we might contribute humbly to generating radical evidence toward transformation. Each essay takes seriously the power relations of the world as it is; the vibrant possibilities of activist research crafted at the membrane of university and community; the knowledge nourished in struggle; the joy of solidarities and the heartbreak of structural violence. Written by emergent activist scholars, and some of us who have been around for a while, this volume is a must-read for those who are engaged in democratic participatory inquiry. Ana and Joy, when neoliberalism penetrates our institutions, despair weighs on our hearts, as crises local and global swell - this is just when we need a movement for just research. As books are being banned; language policed; student dissent criminalized; faculty censored and a new McCarthyism seeps into our academic and community lives, you offer us rich sketches of activist desire, resistance, persistence, solidarities and struggles for a world not yet.

Just when it seems so clear the academy is a colonial institution dedicated to profit and reproduction, we read essays that reveal the liberatory possibilities that erupt/disrupt and re-imagine from within higher education at the luscious border with co.

And you will learn a bit about the amazing life story of URBAN, a trans-institutional network that willed ourselves into being, that has held fierce belief that the academy is accountable to struggles on the ground, that participatory praxis is oxygen to movements for an anti-racist/anti-capitalist world to come.

*—Michelle Fine, Distinguished Professor, CUNY*
*Critical Psychology/Urban Education and Visiting Professor*
*University of South Africa*

This impressive volume highlights the promise of community-engaged scholarship for promoting social justice while demonstrating the vital role that URBAN has played in carving out spaces for this work to thrive. It foregrounds a research approach that builds upon the knowledge of those often excluded from vital conversation and demonstrates how deep connections and engagement among scholars, researchers, practitioners, and community-based organizers can create new possibilities for transformative social change. Everyone committed to community-engaged scholarship, and a more just society should read this book.

*—John Diamond, Professor of Sociology and Education Policy,*
*Brown's Department of Sociology and Annenberg Institute for School Reform*

# All In

## Urban Matters

Ana C. Antunes, Editor

Founded in 2010, the Urban Research Based Action Network (URBAN) is committed to strengthening relationships between academics and community-based practitioners, connecting traditionally siloed issue areas, and creating mechanisms to increase scholarly recognition of this work. While the topics and scope of each volume in this book series will be different, all of them will be linked by the ways in which knowledge production is understood within the network. That means that chapters for each volume are not only written by university faculty but co-written with community partners, undergraduate and graduate students, and youth. We believe that it is our commitment to include voices that are often excluded from academic knowledge production that makes the URBAN Book Series different than other academic series.

**Forthcoming Titles:**

*All In: Community Engaged Scholarship for Social Change*
Edited by Ana C. Antunes and Joy Howard (2024)

If you are interested in submitting a proposal for publication consideration, please send your prospectus to the series editor Ana C. Antunes: ana.antunes@utah.edu

# All In

## Community Engaged Scholarship for Social Change

EDITED BY *Ana C. Antunes and Joy Howard*

*Gorham, Maine*

Published by Myers Education Press, LLC
P.O. Box 424 Gorham, ME 04038



**Myers Education Press** is an academic publisher specializing in books, e-books, and digital content in the field of education. All of our books are subjected to a rigorous peer review process and produced in compliance with the standards of the Council on Library and Information Resources.

Library of Congress Cataloging-in-Publication Data available from Library of Congress.

13-digit ISBN 978-1-9755-0593-6 (paperback)
13-digit ISBN 978-1-9755-0594-3 (library networkable e-edition)
13-digit ISBN 978-1-9755-0595-0 (consumer e-edition)

Printed in the United States of America.

All first editions printed on acid-free paper that meets the American National Standards Institute Z39-48 standard.

Books published by Myers Education Press may be purchased at special quantity discount rates for groups, workshops, training organizations, and classroom usage. Please call our customer service department at 1-800-232-0223 for details.

*Cover design by Teresa Lagrange.*

Visit us on the web at **www.myersedpress.com** to browse our complete list of titles.

# Contents

## List of Figures and Tables

## **Foreword**

# *Jose Calderon*

THE ARTICLES IN this book show how far the Urban Based Action Network has come in building connections between engaged scholars from multiple disciplines in conducting community-based and collaborative forms of research. They follow with the original conception of URBAN (that I was part of as a founder back in 2012) alongside a group of scholars, researchers, and community-based organizers, who sought to advance a type of collaborative research that focused on problems that urban communities were facing. Professor Marilyn Gitell (1931–2010), who originally was part of this group and in whose memory URBAN was organized, exemplified all that URBAN has come to be. She was a scholar-activist who used her research and organizing skills to build multi-racial coalitions and advance racial, gender, and educational justice outcomes in Brooklyn's neighborhood schools.

Together we sought to advance a paradigm that used participatory science and social action research alongside community-based organizations to analyze problems, implement solutions, and advance social change outcomes. And now this anthology is the legacy of those initial organizers where URBAN is helping to fill a gap in "social action writing" where community engagement and research are used for social change outcomes that serve the interests of our communities. This is what stands out in the articles in this anthology where the authors are engaged in the communities and organizations that they are writing about, learning from the implementation of social change strategies, using their writing to build on the lessons learned, and advancing the building of a social movement through networks of such social activist researchers and scholars.

The new and young scholars in this anthology represent a legacy of creating pathways through the requisites of the academic world while gathering both qualitative and quantitative data as lessons that can be built on by community organizers and other activist scholars. Rather than standing from afar, the activist scholars in this anthology are participants in the process of social, political, economic, and quality of life social change. It is the kind of knowledge building that transforms the individual through collective experience. Hence, we have the concrete example of the activist scholar who simultaneously highlights the transformative work of a service-learning organization while sharing how the research and engagement "saved her" and created a place for this type of research and learning in the long term. We have the example of participatory research on wage theft that is not just about defining wage theft and its effects in both the global north and global south, but also how this understanding led to community-based engagement through educational forums and Domestic Workers legislation signed by the governor in California. We have the example of the activist scholar who got involved in union organizing, transformed through taking classes on the history of unions, and conducted research that led to a long-term commitment to union organizing and the use of research as a tool in building unions. We have the uniqueness of research on philanthropy and how social capital can be part of ensuring the long-term sustainability of nonprofits. We have the activist researcher who participated in Californians for Justice protests and legislative campaigns as part of a larger strategy to overcome systemic racism in schools. We have the Indigenous researchers and the application of decolonized intersectional research methods to implement "equity-centred action organizing strategies." And finally we have the activist researcher sharing the lessons of working alongside an environmental justice collective in promoting "food sovereignty and educational justice through agricultural initiatives."

Overall, the articles in this book are about the future in advancing a type of research where there is a passion for social justice and creating spaces of equity. They look at some of the systemic and structural aspects of inequity; bring to center stage the contributions of communities who (because of poverty, racism, sexism, classism, or homophobia) have historically been excluded; and involve researchers in working alongside those communities on common projects to implement transformative social change. The examples in this book are not isolated examples but reflect an ethos of community engagement and community-based research that URBAN has advanced in the last 10 years; an ethos rooted in the building of a multidisciplinary network of research and action for the benefit of community-based organizations and its members; an ethos with the long-term goal of social change and reciprocity; and where community engagement and research are part of a larger program to empower the participants, develop their leadership, and develop the foundations that will allow them to function as active participants in the larger world of policymaking.

This type of community engagement and research leads us in the direction of crossing borders to new models of building democratic participation in our communities and the creation of a more democratic, equitable, and socially just culture in our society.

# Introduction

THIS INITIAL BOOK is an extension of over a decade-long collaboration among scholars, activists, educators, and youth across the United States in Urban Research Based Action Network (URBAN). Our hope is to connect to an even broader audience and to extend an invitation to join us in community-centered work. In this edited volume, authors at various stages of their academic and professional careers, and in very different geographical contexts and community settings, provide unique examples of the ethos of our network. We hope that readers will be able to envision tangible examples of public scholarship for social justice and be inspired to begin, to continue, and to extend their own project within various communities.

The authors featured in this book were invited to write about their work based on presentations they gave at the *All In Conference* in Santa Cruz, CA, in 2022. This conference was the largest URBAN-sponsored gathering to date with 440 attendees and was co-sponsored by The Institute for Social Transformation at the University of California, Santa Cruz. The focus of the convening was on critical public scholarship and its role in working towards social justice. There are two types of chapters featured in this volume. The first are the traditional academic book chapters that describe a research study with the results of the community-engaged project. The second are organizers' perspective essays that are shorter chapters where community organizers share success stories, lessons learned, and/or the benefits and challenges of working with university partners.

We begin the volume with a history of URBAN. When planning the first volume of the series, it felt important to us to contextualize the work not only within academic fields, but also relationally within the network. While there are many professional organizations and networks that focus on university–community engaged scholarship, URBAN sets itself apart for its holistic commitment to its members and partners and to social justice–oriented work.

This book is divided in three organizational sections: *Teaching and Curriculum as Activism, Community Based Research as Social Justice,* and *Policy and/or Networking as Justice Work.* The first section focuses on students' voices and opens with the perspective essay "Love & Liberation" by Mimi Ghosh that focuses on how meaningful service-learning opportunities can have a lifelong impact in the lives of students and highlights the importance of teaching and learning about activism in the higher education context. In "Partnering for Progress: UC Berkeley Students Collaborate with the Asia Floor Wage Alliance (AFWA) to Tackle Garment Industry Wage Theft in the Global South," Zenia Lakhani and Alexis Mullard describe a final course project in which they partnered with Asian trade unions to support human rights in the global supply chains. This chapter focuses on the lessons learned and challenges of transnational allyship and how transnational work can help students connect with heritage cultures and help shape professional futures. Finally, in "The Future of Work/ers through the Pandemic Portal—An Organizer's Perspective," Taylor Valci highlights the benefits and challenges of labor organization and research as an undergraduate student at the university level, in both academic coursework and internship opportunities.

The second section of the book, *Community Based Research as Social Justice,* starts with Angela Frusciante's chapter "Embodying equity through engaged research: A view from within philanthropic initiatives for social change." This chapter analyzes the role of academic knowledge development in connection to nonprofit and philanthropic change strategy. The chapter builds on the growing conversation about the importance of knowledge work for sustainable social change and provides readers with real-life examples of how this works. Next, May Lin's chapter, "How Research Uplifted Youth Visions for Care and Racial Justice in Californians for Justice's Relationship Centered Schools Campaign," highlights how youth-led research in education can drive real change. It does so by focusing on a campaign by the organization *Californians for Justice* on the importance of interpersonal relationships between students and school personnel.

Finally, the third section, *Policy and/or Networking as Justice Work,* begins with "Indigenous Approaches to Equity Research: A Story of California's Central Coast Community" by Morgan Love and colleagues in which they describe the work of the Central Coast Equity Initiative. This chapter highlights a three-year participatory research process that has engaged the Santa Barbara and Ventura communities in understanding and framing equity issues. Next, Paige Bray and Erin Kenney's chapter, "Commitment to Pedagogical Partners in Early Childhood," offers a critical examination of how early childhood practitioners acquire knowledge of equitable practices and work in context-specific communities to implement them. In the last chapter of this section, Adrienne Cachelin and colleagues describe a community collaborative project around food justice in "Embracing the Journey: Growing Educational Pathways for Food Sovereignty." This chapter focuses on food and education justice and how culturally sustaining urban agriculture initiatives can advance school belonging among marginalized students.

We conclude this volume with our closing remarks about community-engaged scholarship. This is followed by an afterword written by Ronald David Glass, who describes the future of the field and what is ahead for the Urban Research Based Action Network.

**CHAPTER 1**

# The History of URBAN

## *Joy Howard and Ana Carolina Antunes*

THIS BOOK IS a natural outgrowth of over a decade of work from a network dedicated to building the field of community engaged activist scholarship. URBAN, or the Urban Research Based Action Network, is made up of activist scholars from diverse fields (e.g., sociology, urban planning, education) who live and work in different contexts (e.g., east coast, west coast, Midwest, urban and even rural settings). They come from higher education spaces, nonprofits, community organizations, and grassroots organizing. In this brief introduction to URBAN, we aim to contextualize how this series came about and why we think it is so important to pull the authors together in this volume. We want to be clear that book is only possible because of the genius and generosity of a host of individuals and groups. These are people who have united efforts to work toward justice efforts in communities and schools across the United States.

We begin this chapter by offering a brief history of URBAN followed by concrete examples of community engaged activist scholarship that has been produced in connection with this collective effort. Finally, we offer a transparent explanation of why we, the editors, pursued this book series and why we are dedicated to highlighting the work of the scholar activists featured herein.

## History

It is hard to say when URBAN actually began. Beginnings are often departures from and revisions of what has come before—and URBAN is a network that embodies the knowledge, skill, efforts, creativity, spirit, and body of work that defies any simplified starting point. With that said, we acknowledge that there are many versions to the beginning of this story and this version represents a collective remembrance of several of us who have been written into the larger story of URBAN over the years.

The Urban Research Action Network was formally started in 2011 to honor the legacy of activist scholar Marylin Gittell. Gittell was a professor of political science at the Graduate Center of the City University in New York and a lifelong advocate for the New York public school system (Fox, 2010). The initial working group of scholars and activists was established with the help of the Miller-McCune Center for Research, Media and Public Policy and SAGE Publications. This group sought to create "living laboratories for hands-on, community-based research that grapples with critical issues emerging in cities and proposes innovative policy solutions to advance social equity" (MIT-Colab, 2012). Though scholars who participated in this initial working group were spread across the United States, with representatives from Los Angeles and Chicago, the majority of URBAN's presence was restricted to the northeast region.

In 2012, the network was formally launched with the support of Dayna Cunningham, SAGE Publications, and Sara McCune with the intention to integrate activists, artists, and scholars as part of a collective struggle for justice and an insistence that universities must serve the public. With the formal launch of the network, its founding members released a working document outlining the objectives of the network. In the document they envisioned national growth that would happen through local "nodes." The objective of the nodes was to promote local solutions to systemic problems and to connect local efforts with those working across the country on similar issues.

The story of URBAN as a national network could be said to have publicly launched at the 2012 American Educational Research Association (AERA) conference in Vancouver, British Columbia. For readers unfamiliar with AERA conferences, the organization is exceedingly big, and to simplify the ways participants find others with similar academic interests, the organization is divided into special interest groups (SIGs). Several founders of one of those groups, the Grassroots Community Youth Organizing (GCYO) SIG, began a discussion about how AERA members and conference participants could unite to encourage, support, and model how scholars can work in deep partnership with community organizers and educational activists to conduct research in support of racial equity and social justice. Involved in these conversations were members of the URBAN working group (e.g., Mark Warren, Ron Glass) formed the previous year on the East Coast.

The next year, in 2013, some of the activist scholars who were part of the GCYO met at a union hall (due to a union boycott of the conference hotel) in San Francisco during AERA. As a result of this meeting, organized by Mark Warren, Ronald Glass, and Jerusha Conner, the URBAN education node (which we now refer to ask the education collective) was launched as a branch of the URBAN Research-Based Action Network. The educational node became a branch of the larger network. URBAN has insisted that public universities take seriously our public praxis commitment to movements, critique, aesthetic provocation, and radical possibilities.

With mounting interest in related projects and the common commitments we had to justice, especially within marginalized communities, the network has grown through strategic planning and intentional network building. For example, each year since 2015, the national planning team has met with the overarching purpose of building the field of engaged scholarship. The national planning team met to strategize our collective vision and plans at City University of New York (CUNY) in 2015 and 2016 and at Rutgers in 2017. Many of the leaders in this effort are included in the photograph in Figure 1.1.

**Figure 1.1:**
A Few Members of the URBAN National Planning Team (Right to left, Steve McKay, Ana Antunes, Joy Howard, Jennifer Eik, Blanca Trejo, Julio Camarotta, Mark Warren, and Tim Eatman)

## Examining the Past

Connecting scholarship and activism in authentic ways is tricky at best and can even be dangerous. To illustrate the multiple forms this work has taken on, we will illustrate some concrete examples of where, what, and how we have worked together to move our thinking and action forward. This takes the form of conferences, professional development, virtual spaces, and meetings to organize and share our energy and knowledge to build individual and collective capacity to engage with communities through scholarly contributions. We have done this through conferences, professional development, and publications. In this section, we will review some of these efforts.

### *Conferences*

In the early years of URBAN, there was a lot of effort to build collaborative spaces at national conferences in our unique fields. For example, the URBAN education node planning team worked together to organize and co-sponsor events and sessions at the AERA and the American Sociological Association for several years. This involved putting together a broad range of Presidential sessions, symposia, papers, intentional collaborative offerings with graduate students, and off-site sessions (see our website, https://urbanresearchnetwork.org/, for more activities and publicly available manuscripts). The objective of being in these field-specific conferences has focused on supporting local community activist organizations by (1) building community-engaged research networks across towns and cities; (2) grappling with ethical tensions in university community-engaged scholarship; (3) providing mentorship opportunities among senior, junior, and graduate student activist scholars; and (4) establishing national solidarities on behalf of pushing back unjust neoliberal reforms impacting schools, cities, and all kinds of rural, urban, and suburban communities.

Beyond field-specific gatherings, as mentioned above, URBAN has hosted four interdisciplinary conferences across the country since 2015. The first two URBAN conferences, organized by Mark Warren, were hosted at the University of Massachusetts in Boston. The first conference, entitled *Collaborative Research for Equity and Action in Education,* focused on five topics: (1) Advocacy, Neutrality, and Collaborative, Equity-oriented Research Practices; (2) Collaborative

Research; (3) Critical Participatory Policy/Organizing; (4) Ethical Issues in Collaborative Social Science Research; and (5) Institutional Supports for Collaborative Research. Participants of the conference published their discussions and resolutions in a special issue of the journal *Urban Education*. The second Boston conference was held with the support of the W.T. Grant Foundation and the Spencer Foundation. While the first Boston conference focused on theory and academic practice, the second focused on highlighting community organizing efforts like New York's Morris Project and Boston's Youth Hub.

In 2016 Celina Su organized the third URBAN conference, entitled *Critical Solidarities and Multi-Scalar Power,* at the Graduate Center at City University of New York (CUNY). The 2016 event focused on the "right to research," who owns community data, and how those get used as social networks and safety nets become a "complex web of decentralized private-public partnerships [and] multinational corporations." In 2018, the URBAN Colorado Node, spearheaded by Ben Kirshner and Antwan Jefferson, organized a conference called *Place and Displacement: Towards Building and Sustaining Just Communities,* which highlighted scholars' and activists' efforts to build and sustain research partnerships that address issues of place and displacement, centering in particular gentrification of Black and nonwhite neighborhoods. The conference was funded by the Spencer Foundation, which allowed for a group of participants to return to Denver in the fall of 2018 to develop an issue for The Assembly—A journal for public scholarship on education that focused on connecting cross-country activism that targeted similar issues.

Our goal of organizing a conference every 2 years was derailed, like many other things, by the COVID-19 pandemic. URBAN was originally scheduled to convene in Santa Cruz, California, in April 2020, but the conference only happened in October of 2022. Despite its delay, or perhaps because of it, the *All In Santa Cruz* conference was the largest to date with 440 attendees. The conference was co-sponsored by The Institute For Social Transformation at the University of California, Santa Cruz and was centered around critical public scholarship and its role in working towards social justice.

While the pandemic stopped us from meeting in person for a three-year stretch, URBAN strengthened its network virtually during this time. For example, we co-hosted several free book clubs featuring Leigh Patel and Jamilya Lyiscott during summer months open to anyone who was interested. In 2020, we organized two webinars—Community Based Research Navigating the Turbulent Time and

Places of Political and Biological Pandemics in Contentious Times: Some Reflections. In 2021 we focused on the theme Seizing the Pandemic Portal: Transforming Universities for Community Engaged Scholarship and organized another virtual event to discuss the topic. In 2022 we began an URBAN Matters series that included a variety of relevant topics in an online forum (see https://urbanresearchnetwork.org/ for more in-depth information).

### *Professional Development and Training Opportunities*

Beyond the network-building efforts at conferences and guided online dialogue, URBAN leaders have organized professional development activities as an investment in our collective capacity building. For example, in 2016 the Education strand of URBAN offered a preconference participatory research workshop prior to the AERA conference and a workshop session specifically aimed at supporting dissertation work that utilized community-based participatory action research (PAR). In 2017, the same group offered two virtual participatory research workshops about PAR and Human Rights in Education as well as a fireside chat at AERA about community engagement and PAR approaches to research. These types of sessions in virtual spaces and at site-based locations (e.g., Urban Research Based Action Network Meeting on Community-Engaged Scholarship @ASA 2019) have continued to grow over the years.

Presently, our efforts are directed at creating a framework for URBAN Matters that will include virtual spaces for learning and sharing skills and knowledge in justice-oriented community-engaged scholarship. This book series is an investment in creating texts that will support and document the diverse approaches and outcomes of the efforts of scholar-activists who continue to push the field forward.

### *Publications*

Anyone who is or has been a part of academia is aware that peer-reviewed publications are an important part of scholarship and sharing ideas broadly. Therefore, URBAN scholars have collaborated on several published works, including a special issue in the *International Journal of Qualitative Studies in Education* (2016). This special issue included the work of Nicole Mirra, Allyson

Tintiangco-Cubales, Korina Jocson, and Antwi Akom. Another special issue in *Urban Education* (2018) included the work of Mark Warren, John Diamond, Timothy Eatman, Michelle Fine, and Ron Glass. Important contributions were also collected in the *Educational Policy Analysis Archives* (2019) that included articles by Celina Su and Maria Elena Torre among many others. Mark Warren and David Goodman's book *Lift Us Up Don't Push Us Out* demonstrates a diverse group of scholar activists from both inside and outside the academy writing about educational justice. Chapter authors include contributions by Natasha Capers, Vajra Watson, practicing teachers and activists, and Jose Calderon. Although it is not possible to write out a comprehensive list of all the work that URBAN scholars have produced (both in scholarly journals and community-endorsed publications and resources), we have noted some recent publications that may be of interest to readers at the end of this chapter.

## Field-Building to Date

Altogether, we have engaged in field building efforts for more than a decade to ask critical questions about the role of scholarship and research in coalition building with communities as a means to create positive change where injustice abounds. This speaks to what Mark Warren calls collaborative community engaged scholarship (CCES). As Warren describes, CCES involves a partnership between the community and educational activists as a means to create knowledge in direct support of equity-oriented changed agendas (Warren, 2018). This umbrella term is inclusive of a range of disciplines and methodologies, including PAR, YPAR, action research, community-based research, and CBPAR. It is not limited to educational or school settings alone; rather it is inclusive of education-related research collaborations in the community. URBAN's focus then is largely to advance the field of CCES among and between like-minded scholars from a variety of disciplines, geographical contexts, and methodological preferences with equity at the center of all of our efforts.

Describing the scope and form of URBAN has been an ongoing challenge because it is ever evolving in nature; however, as a group we have proposed a few useful metaphors. One way to understand our collaborative work has been as an archipelago or a constellation, where our collective projects are simultaneously unified by equity and at the same time diverse and autonomous (URBAN

National, 2017). There are clear challenges of funding a national project, organizing across spaces and bridging communication gaps across time and place, so it is an evolving work in process.

We have made some strategic moves to expand the reach of our network. For example, at our 2018 URBAN national meeting at Rutgers, we determined that the American Educational Studies Association would be a generative space to not only share our work, but to invite like-minded scholars to join this ongoing conversation about field building in collaborative community engaged scholarship and equity-oriented partnerships with/in the communities where we gather, live, and/or do our work. As a whole, URBAN takes up the work of critical race praxis and invites academics, activists and academic-activists, graduate students and faculty alike, to join in the work. We are strengthened by diverse representation of academic-activists who represent unique regional and local perspectives on issues of structural violence and radical possibilities that affect localized attacks on communities that too often go unquestioned given the trends of privatization and the commodification of K-12 schools and universities.

## Re-imagining the Future

In recent years, largely due to pandemic-related concerns and institutional changes, the work has necessarily evolved. While the isolation of the pandemic was hard on all of us, the URBAN Network found ways to continue to build community and learn from each other. URBAN leaders and participants have begun to meet regularly via Zoom and other technologies that allow us to regularly check in. Notably, the tenor and expectations of our meetings breaks from the norms of many academic spaces. While most of the leadership team are in higher education, there is intentionality around diversity of voice. In other words, some leaders have been graduate students while others are tenured faculty and others are senior administrators of programs and departments at their respective universities. There is an expectation of care where laughter is expected, we make space for grief, and hope is passed along to share.

Additionally, the pandemic also created opportunities for us to imagine URBAN differently. With the support of the Robert Wood Johnson Foundation, since 2023 URBAN has focused its efforts to build capacity for community organizers, scholars, and funding officers interested in learning more about community engaged scholarship. One of the ways we are achieving this goal is to make community-engaged research and praxis available for a wider audience. This book series is part of this effort.

The URBAN Matters Book Series is one of the three prongs of URBAN Matters, which also includes a blog and virtual talks. We hope that beyond engaging with the chapters in this book, readers will find their way into the different spaces that we have created to support scholars and activists who share commitments to just education and just research as a means to create a more socially just world.

## Recent Publications

- *Social Sciences Journal,* 2022 Special Issue "New Trends in Community-Engaged Research: Co-producing Knowledge for Justice"
- *The Assembly,* 2022 URBAN Special Issue (result of the Colorado Conference in 2018)
- *Education Policy Analysis Archives* 27, 2019 Collaborative research and multi-issue movement building for educational justice: Reflections on the Urban Research Based Action Network (URBAN)
- *Urban Education* 53, 4 Special Issue: Building the Emerging Field of Collaborative, Community Engaged Education Research
- Balaram, A (2018) Defining and Conceptualizing Human Rights for Community-Engaged Research & Action https://urbanresearchnetwork.org/defining-and-conceptualizing-human-rights-for-community-engaged-research-action-by-arita-balaram/
- *International Journal of Qualitative Studies in Education* 29, 10 Special Issue: Challenging Neoliberal Reforms through Collaborative, Community Engaged Research
- *Critical Sociology* 41, 7-8 URBAN Special Issue

- Guidelines for Peer-Reviewing Community-Based Research https://www.asanet.org/wp-content/uploads/guidelines-for-peer-review-of-community-based-research.pdf

## References


Fox, M. (2010). Marilyn Gittell, Advocate for Local School Decision, Dies at 78. *The New York Times*. Retrieved: https://www.nytimes.com/2010/03/13/nyregion/13 gittell.html

MIT-Colab (2012). *URBAN: Concept Paper*. Retrieved from: https://web.mit.edu/colab/pdf/work/urban-booklet.pdf

URBAN National (2017). 2017 URBAN Retreat Notes. Internal document.

Warren, M. R. (2018). Research confronts equity and social justice–building the emerging field of collaborative, community engaged education research: Introduction to the special issue. *Urban Education, 53*(4), 439–444.

# Section I

## Teaching and Curriculum as Activism

**Chapter 2**

# Love & Liberation

## *Mimi Ghosh*

> *"The programs of the Service Learning Institute engage the content, practice, and pedagogy of service learning to promote social transformation and create a more just world."*
>
> — Seth Pollack, Former SLI Director

Getting to attend CSU Monterey Bay was an almost insurmountable task on its own. I faced an upward struggle with a financial aid system designed to keep students in the dark about the resources available to them. I was 17 years old with no familial support, no driver's license, and only a few hundred dollars to my name saved from working at my hometown boba shop. Because my dad was a CEO, I didn't qualify for any financial aid but I knew attending university was my only hope of escaping my dysfunctional household. I fought tooth and nail to find any means to separate myself from my parents' income and finally discovered the existence of the Dependency Override Form. Using this form as a foothold I was able to get loans for university but my job at the Service Learning Institute was integral to keeping me in school while also helping me pay for it.

With the support of Dr. Pamela Motoike, faculty coordinator of the Student Leadership program at the time, I was able to make my dreams a reality one step at a time. I currently hold a B.A. in Humanities and Communications with a concentration in Legal Studies and a minor in Social Justice and Community Leadership. At a time in my life when I needed it, Pam believed in me. Despite only getting a C+ in her class, she saw something in me. She hired me as the youngest Service Learning Student Leader to be given the opportunity to co-teach a service learning course. Dr. Chrissy Hernandez and I were paired together. Under Chrissy's guidance, I helped teach the service learning course The Promise and Reality of the American Dream: Feminisms & Social Justice. My prior education in women's studies helped me rise to this challenge. I continued to teach different service learning courses over the next 4 years.

Cal State Monterey Bay is the only public university in the state of California to make service learning a graduation requirement. Undergraduate students at CSU Monterey Bay complete two service learning courses during their bachelor's degree program, one lower division course and one upper division course. In my position as a Service Learning Student Leader representing the Service Learning Institute of CSU Monterey Bay, I presented at the *All-In: Co-Creating Knowledge for Justice* conference held in picturesque Santa Cruz, California. On my panel, I spoke about the value of the Service Learning Student Leadership Program and the importance of service learning to both university students and the community as a whole. To provide a holistic view of the Service Learning Student Leadership Program, in this chapter I will explain my experiences in the program and describe my perspectives on the impact of my work supported by the Service Learning Institute.

A Service Learning Student Leader works to bridge the gap between community partners and service learning students at CSU Monterey Bay. Service Learning Student Leaders have two different roles, community-based student leaders and course-based student leaders. Community-based student leaders are placed at different community partner sites and work throughout the year to become a liaison between students and people in community sites. As a course-based student leader, I was paired with a service learning professor and placed in a college classroom. I gave my own lectures, led activities, provided feedback on essays, and supported my students however they needed me.

During my first semester of freshman year at Cal State Monterey Bay, I completed the university lower division service learning requirement. In a class called The Promise and Reality of the American Dream, I worked on unpacking systemic racism, understanding intersectional social identities, and finding my own definition of what service learning meant to me. Along with learning the theories and texts that help us understand critical service learning, we were also taught how to reflect on the engagement hours we were completing outside of our class.

The Central Coast Citizenship Project was the community site I worked with during that semester. To help us get familiarized with the different opportunities available to us as service learning students, my professor set up a number of community partner presentations. At the Central Coast Citizenship Project, students would help immigrants of mostly Mexican background study for and pass their U.S. citizenship tests. My own parents immigrated from Kolkata, India, to California in the 1990s, and as a young girl, I remember seeing them studying for their citizenship test, quizzing each other from their study guides. We all celebrated when they both passed their tests. Given my personal connection to the issue, along with my deep love of American history and government, I knew this setting would be the best place to complete my service learning engagement hours.

Have you ever tasted payesh? How about arroz con leche? When any of the students at the Central Coast Citizenship Project would pass their test, we had a lovely tradition of bringing in food and taking the day off to celebrate. One day a student brought in little cups and handed them out after he passed his test. I took a bite and to my absolute surprise, I was transported back to eating homemade payesh on every birthday celebration from my childhood. Thoroughly confused, I asked if this was payesh, a sweet Bengali rice pudding very close to my heart. The group explained that no, it was arroz con leche, a Mexican rice pudding with a sprinkle of cinnamon on top. I couldn't believe it. My whole life I had thought that payesh was strictly Indian and here I was surrounded by a new community far away from home still feeling that same connection.

Diversity is built into the very fabric of our country. It's what makes America so unique, a true melting pot of people and cultures. Communities across the nation may look starkly different from one another but there are ties between us connecting us not only to each other but to the land that we are stewards of. That moment of tasting my first ever bite of arroz con leche has forever reminded me that we are so much more alike than we are different. We may look different and our communities may face different challenges but at the core of our humanity, the love between us is the same. We all define what it means to be an American differently. It was one of the first questions I was asked in my service learning class. This is one of my favorite anecdotes because it helps me answer that question. I am incredibly blessed to be able to share this story with my students each semester.

Despite where I am in my service learning journey now, it took a while to discover the program at my university that could both utilize my gifts and also turn into a strong career path. I attribute my dissonance to being in the wrong major for too long. I ended up in Business, not in Legal Studies which is my real passion, in part due to discouragement from a pessimistic history professor. Looking for some guidance, I explained my situation and my dreams and he told me that due to the competitive nature of the profession, I would never get a job as a university professor. In front of a class full of students at orientation, he drew a fraction on the whiteboard, 1/247, the number of hires out of a pool of applicants, still seared into my brain years later.

Having been told no at every turn and barely clawing my way into university in the first place, his harsh words scared me into changing my major to business. I was paying for school on my own and with no idea what my life would look like after college, I settled on a more practical major that I thought could get me a job right out of my undergrad. Looking back now, that professor was wrong to discourage me, especially because so many other professors have believed in me since. I keep that experience in mind now, making sure I present information differently to my own college classes. Today I know that there are all kinds of programs and support systems to guide students through their educational journey. I make sure to highlight different avenues through which my students can pursue their goals and find resources that will support them. Although that professor had made me and my dreams feel insignificant, my community at the Service Learning Institute made me feel unstoppable. Less than a year after hearing that I was never going to teach politics at the college level, here I was doing it, living my dream at 18 while still in my undergrad.

The Service Learning Student Leadership Program changed the course of my life in the best ways possible. For the past 4 years, it has given me a way to put myself through college while also developing personal and professional skills. I have presented at conferences at Cal Poly SLO, UC Berkeley, and UC Santa Cruz. I've also connected with over a hundred students in my six different classes and found a career path that truly fits me. This was all possible because of the incredible people we have at the Service Learning Institute who believed in me so much that I started believing in myself. The pathways that I am considering after graduation all help create institutional change at a federal level. Dr. Chrissy Hernandez led our summer retreat training and focused our learning on prison abolition. I was also lucky enough to be in attendance at the keynote address that Dr. Angela Davis gave on the same topic at the Change the Status Quo Conference at Cal Poly SLO. I took my learning to the local high schools in Monterey and gave students a presentation on the school-to-prison pipeline. To continue my advocacy work in the same field, I would like to work for organizations such as Dream.org that focus on ending mass incarceration and creating racial justice.

One of the best parts of the leadership program is it gives back as much as you are willing to put in. Outside the classroom and the daily scope of my duties, the faculty coordinator of the student leadership program always informed us of conference opportunities we could apply to present at. If I had something to say and the desire to be heard there was always a way to make that happen. That's how I got the opportunity to present at the *All-In: Co-Creating Knowledge for Justice* conference and was offered the opportunity to be a part of this book today. My boss, Chrissy, also guided me in applying to present at the same *Change the Status Quo* conference at Cal Poly SLO that we all attended the year prior. I volunteered with a grassroots organization called Renegade Feedings in my hometown of Fremont. With the knowledge from both of my communities, I created a workshop called *Building Community: Deconstructing the Stigma Around Homelessness & Creating Meaningful Change*. My job with the Service Learning Student Leadership Program gave me a platform to share the knowledge I had collected from different people in different communities. In my workshop, I presented them with the tools I had learned and they immediately started co-creating knowledge themselves, exchanging phone numbers and local organizations in the Zoom chat. It was incredible to see people come together and breathe life into a shared cause. Together, the people in attendance became a living breathing example of the change we were trying to create.

The community in Monterey comes together through service learning at the university. On our winter work retreat, we went out to visit a grassroots nonprofit organization, The Monterey Peace and Justice Center. To give an example of just how deep the connections flow and the community ties run, I'll tell you about the sweetest present I've ever received. The volunteers at the Monterey Peace and Justice Center were all older; one of them had been fighting for justice since she was a teenager protesting the Vietnam War. After the formal presentation, I spoke to one of the volunteers alone. She was a soft older

Asian lady who reminded me of my own grandmother. I learned about her decades of work and admired a beautiful necklace she had on. She told me how the beads of the colorful necklace were made of paper. Before I could protest, with loving and weathered hands she took the necklace off and placed it around my neck to keep. That kindness is what service is to me. That community is what being American means to me. I serve my community with love, a love so strong for people I may not know simply because the wholeness in us connects to the wholeness in them. As much as the Service Learning Institute is four brick and mortar walls with a beautiful mural and a mosaic out front, it is also a sense of safety, community, and home.

**CHAPTER 3**

# Partnering for Progress: UC Berkeley Students Collaborate with the Asia Floor Wage Alliance (AFWA) to Tackle Garment Industry Wage Theft in the Global South

*Zenia Lakhani and Alexis Mullard*

IN THIS CHAPTER, we conduct a thorough analysis of our collaborative project with the Asia Floor Wage Alliance (AFWA), offering a comprehensive exploration of the transformative impact of community engagement in labor rights advocacy and its potential impact on addressing wage theft. Our research investigated the pervasive issue of wage theft, making connections between the practices of global corporations and the persistent wage theft experienced by garment workers at the bottom of their supply chains. We also explored the struggles faced by the U.S. labor movement, examining demands formulated during minimum wage struggles and identifying effective organizing, campaigning, and bargaining strategies. By understanding these experiences, our goal was to extract insights to enhance the AFWA's efforts in the fight against wage theft. Here we use the definition of wage theft as one that encompasses various forms of wage theft, including minimum wage violations, overtime violations, off-the-clock work, illegal deductions, and misclassification of employees.

The initial section lays the foundation by defining the concept of community engagement and highlighting its empowering role in amplifying the voices of workers and local communities. We emphasize the significance of community engagement in increasing issue visibility, compelling key stakeholders to advocate for policy change. Building upon this understanding, we then delve into the specifics of our partnership with the AFWA, illustrating how collaboration at the local level can foster enduring change within the global garment industry. An emphasis is placed on the importance of leveraging the UC Berkeley's unique perspectives and resources for social justice initiatives. Addressing the challenges of international work, we also outline effective strategies for fostering community engagement in labor rights advocacy.

## Authors' Positionality

Throughout her early undergraduate years, Zenia prioritized fulfilling medical school requirements, driven by her aspiration to serve her community as a physician. However, her perspective took a transformative turn when she enrolled in a seminar on Social, Political, and Ethical Issues in Health and Medicine, which exposed her to the stark interconnectedness of government policy, socioeconomic status, and health disparities within communities. This provided a platform for Zenia to explore the ethical and social aspects of health and medicine, challenging her to look beyond the traditional medical framework. Eager to delve deeper into the societal factors influencing health outcomes, Zenia decided to pursue a minor in Public Policy, immersing herself in the study of policy-making processes and their impact on communities. The course discussed in this chapter, entitled Collaborative Innovation, further fueled Zenia's interest in collaborative approaches to address complex societal issues, cementing her conviction that combining medicine and policy is crucial for effecting change in healthcare systems.

With a Bachelor of Arts in Interdisciplinary Studies from UC Berkeley, specializing in Sustainable Design, Circular Fashion, Entrepreneurship, Business, and Technology, Alexis is dedicated to creating a more sustainable fashion industry. Through extensive research, Alexis has focused on utilizing blockchain technology to transition to a more sustainable and circular system in fashion, aiming to bring transparency, traceability, authenticity, and accountability to fashion brands. Alexis is committed to collaborative innovation and exploring the intersection of multiple disciplines. Alexis is also actively involved in addressing labor rights issues in the global garment industry, working with the AFWA and UC Berkeley students to combat wage theft and promote fair labor practices. Through her work, she seeks to protect the well-being of workers in the fashion industry while striving to protect the environment and promote social and environmental justice in the fashion industry.

The Collaborative Innovation course at UC Berkeley serves as a catalyst in the fight for justice by addressing real-world challenges and fostering collaborative efforts. Led by a diverse team of faculty from the departments of public policy, business, and theater, dance, and performance studies, the course embraces a multidisciplinary approach to problem-solving and innovation. It encourages students to think critically and explore creative avenues such as design thinking to drive meaningful change.

Ultimately, the culmination of this course was a final project in which students were partnered with community organizations to utilize their newly honed collaborative innovation skills and produce corresponding deliverables. We were given the opportunity to partner with the AFWA, each drawn to the organization for our own compelling reasons. For Zenia the AFWA's work in combating human rights violations in her native countries, Pakistan and Bangladesh, struck a deeply personal chord—especially given that her uncle is currently the proprietor of multiple factories in Bangladesh. She wanted to understand the root cause of the labor violations taking place in her countries, as well as learn about the ways in which she can serve as an advocate for change. On the other hand, Alexis was driven by her passion for sustainable fashion and her vision for a more transparent, circular fashion system. Our collaboration allowed us to apply our unique perspectives, consolidate concrete research and evidence, and work towards systemic change, envisioning a more just future for workers in global supply chains.

## *The Asia Floor Wage Alliance*

Founded in 2006, the AFWA is composed of over 76 organizations, including garment industry trade unions, NGOs, consumer groups, and research groups from over 17 countries across Asia, Europe, and North America. The alliance focuses on demanding living wages for garment workers while addressing poverty-level wages, gender discrimination, and freedom of association in global garment production networks. The AFWA's primary efforts are centered in India, Pakistan, Bangladesh, Indonesia, Sri Lanka, and Cambodia, where the garment industry plays a significant role in the economy. This organization's intention for proposing a collaborative project was to utilize the perspectives of UC Berkeley students, backed by an arsenal of consolidated concrete research and evidence, to support and strengthen the strategies utilized by Asian trade union efforts. The AFWA recognizes the urgent need for systemic change to enhance workers' rights in the garment industry. One of their notable initiatives involves pursuing legal action against global clothing brands, advocating for these retailers to be legally considered joint employers alongside suppliers. This approach aims to hold brands accountable for wage violations, particularly during the COVID-19 pandemic when instances of wage theft escalated dramatically.

Our collaborative project with the AFWA embodies a dedicated effort to tackle the obstacles hindering an equitable future for workers in global supply chains. Through the thorough exploration of the concept of wage theft from diverse perspectives, analysis of key learnings from case studies, and assessment of the impact of the COVID-19 crisis's impact on both the Global North and Global South, we were able to make a valuable comparison between the presence of wage theft in more developed countries and its rampant prevalence among garment workers in the Global South. Our collaborative effort with the AFWA sought to develop a comprehensive concept of "wage theft" that could serve as a potent tool for union advocacy and bargaining efforts. Our aim was to produce a well-defined and impactful definition of wage theft, which could be used to hold global fashion labels and top retailers accountable for potential rights violations, particularly in the scope of the pandemic era. Our objective was to provide the AFWA with valuable insights into strategies utilized to combat wage theft in the Global North, which could be adapted to bolster their current approach in advocating for government regulation of the global garment labor landscape.

### *Challenges to International Work*

As UC Berkeley students collaborating with the AFWA to address the widespread problem of wage theft in the global garment industry, we embarked on an eye-opening journey that presented us with both valuable insights and significant challenges. Throughout this endeavor, one of the most prominent hurdles we encountered was the vast gap in communication caused by time differences and language barriers. Being continents apart, conducting interviews with the workers proved to be a formidable task, hindering our ability to gain firsthand insights into their experiences. Nevertheless, our determination to shed light on their struggles persisted, and we remained committed to finding alternative means to address this critical issue. Instead of direct interviews, we turned to the AFWA's Instagram videos, where we discovered a collection of worker stories vividly depicting the daily hardships they endured. These videos proved to be invaluable resources for our research, as they allowed us to gain deep insights into the real challenges faced by these workers within the industry. We utilized the available videos to craft each worker profile to highlight these individuals' unique and shared experiences. We intended to present an authentic representation of their lives, shedding light on the harsh realities they confront regularly. One advantage of using Instagram videos was that they had been shared with the workers' permission, enabling us to use them ethically. Through this process, we sought to emphasize the profound struggles faced by garment workers in the global industry, advocating for change and raising awareness about the issue of wage theft.

The collaboration with AFWA presented us with formidable obstacles, underscoring the intricate nature of addressing systemic problems. Despite these challenges, both parties demonstrated resilience, creativity, and a strong commitment to driving meaningful change. Our primary mode of communication with AFWA was through email, given the vast time differences, but we also engaged in Zoom video calls to ensure a seamless collaboration. Together, we focused on amplifying the voices of garment workers, taking steps toward a future defined by justice and equity. AFWA's involvement showcased the potential of innovative approaches, with us leveraging technology to gather garment worker narratives. This not only enhanced our understanding of pressing issues like wage theft in the industry but also emphasized the significance of overcoming communication and research barriers to achieving our objectives.

### *Strengthening Advocacy in the Global Garment Industry Through Community Engagement*

As we embarked on our journey to shed light on the pressing issue of wage theft in the global garment industry, the initial phase of our project consisted of rigorous research, data analysis, and attempts to obtain firsthand information from garment workers in the Global South. Although we were ultimately unable to directly interview the garment workers themselves due to a language barrier and geographical distance, we did have access to video accounts from garment workers provided by the AFWA. Hearing their stories gave us valuable insights into the complexities of wage theft and its impact on workers' lives. Drawing from our findings, we decided to approach the issue from a different angle by utilizing community engagement as a powerful tool for raising awareness and driving change. Our joint project with the AFWA resulted in the creation of educational pamphlets aimed at educating individuals from all walks of life to comprehend the challenges faced by garment workers and advocate for policy change.

Recognizing that academic research alone might not be enough to create lasting change, we leveraged community engagement as a means to bridge the gap between research findings and public awareness. We understood that to influence market demand, drive government regulation, and motivate brands to take responsibility for their suppliers' labor rights, we needed to engage with the broader population. Thus, we developed educational pamphlets, distributing them in local community centers, around our school, and across various social media platforms, ensuring they reached students, professionals, and everyday consumers. Our educational pamphlets served as a powerful medium to communicate our research findings effectively and inspire individuals to join the advocacy efforts for fair treatment and just wages for garment workers. Through this project, we aimed to strengthen advocacy in the global garment industry and create a ripple effect that extends beyond our academic pursuits.

### *Understanding Community Engagement*

The concept of community engagement encompasses the active participation and involvement of individuals within a community, coming together to address shared challenges and common goals. Community engagement goes beyond passive participation; rather, it seeks the creation of genuine connections, as well as the sharing of ideas between individuals (Levin et al., 2021). The strategic process of community engagement has the ability to empower stakeholders to become active agents of change. We have witnessed the true potential of community engagement in advocating for social justice and equity, particularly in the context of labor rights advocacy in the fashion industry. In our case, it involved uniting students, garment workers, and local communities to tackle labor rights violations in the fashion industry.

Through collective action, we recognized that community engagement provides a powerful platform for advocating social justice and equity. By including the perspectives of those who have been directly affected by labor rights violations, such as garment workers, community engagement amplifies the urgency of addressing systemic issues. By bringing together diverse perspectives, expertise, and resources, we are able to develop comprehensive solutions that resonate with the lived experiences of those subjected to the problem at hand. Thus, inclusive participation is the key to achieving long lasting, sustainable change, while simultaneously demanding stakeholder accountability to advocate for change.

Harnessing the power of community engagement enabled us to gain deeper insights into the challenges faced by garment workers and their local communities. By bridging the gap between academic research and public awareness, our educational pamphlets empowered individuals to become informed advocates for change.

## The Role of Community Engagement in Empowering Workers and Local Communities

Our partnership with the AFWA underscored the profound role that community engagement plays in empowering both workers and local communities. Community engagement served as a catalyst for educating and raising awareness of labor rights violations in the Global South (Levin et al., 2021). Our creation of educational pamphlets proved to be an accessible and effective means of disseminating vital information regarding wage theft in the garment industry. The materials not only shed light on the plight of garment workers but also inspired a wave of compassion and responsibility among individuals. As the pamphlets reached a wider audience, we witnessed a growing movement of informed and empathetic individuals willing to demand ethical practices from fashion brands. For example, we saw tangible outcomes like university students boycotting brands with unethical labor practices and turning to more ethically produced alternatives. Our journey exemplifies how community engagement can promote collective action and challenge existing norms, establishing a more just and equitable future for all stakeholders involved.

The impact of community engagement was far-reaching. By amplifying the voices of those most affected, we began to dismantle the structures that perpetuated labor rights violations and inequality. Our collaborative efforts laid a solid foundation for a more just and sustainable global garment industry. Our vision encompasses a future where workers' rights are safeguarded, their working conditions improved, and their dignity preserved. The transformative potential of community engagement in labor rights advocacy cannot be overstated; it serves as a guiding light in the pursuit of a fair and equitable world for all. The collective action driven by an informed and impassioned community brought to light the severity of this exploitative practice and its pervasive presence within the industry. Our experiences as UC Berkeley students taught us that addressing wage theft requires a comprehensive approach beyond academia's confines.

### *UC Berkeley Students and the AFWA: A Partnership for Change*

In pursuit of advancing workers' rights and fostering a just future of work in global supply chains, we conducted an in-depth exploration of wage theft, dissecting its various definitions and implications. Our analysis encompassed the assessment of the COVID-19 crisis's impact on garment workers, highlighting the challenges they encountered amidst the pandemic's disruptions. In addition, we meticulously studied relevant case studies, drawing key learnings and making meaningful comparisons between practices in more developed countries and the pervasive wage theft experienced by garment workers in the Global South. By connecting the actions of global corporations, including U.S.-based fashion brands, to the persistent wage theft in Asia, we aimed to bring attention to the systemic issues plaguing the garment industry. Factors such as intricate supply chains, price-driven competition, reliance on low-cost labor, and the lack of transparency and regulation have perpetuated the problem of wage theft. The COVID-19 pandemic exacerbated this phenomenon, as brands avoided legal responsibility for the well-being of those involved in garment production.

With a desire to make meaningful contributions to the pursuit of fair and just conditions for garment workers, as well as to increase our understanding of the challenges and possible solutions to combat wage theft, we decided to incorporate the exploration of the struggles faced by the United States labor movement into our research. In this pursuit, we delved into the struggles faced by the U.S. labor movement, extracting invaluable insights and tactics that could be applied more broadly to combat wage theft. A summary of our findings was relayed within our educational pamphlet, in a readily digestible manner; the purpose of communicating the findings in such an accessible manner was rooted in the notion that community engagement increases issue visibility, which ultimately plays a critical role in influencing principal stakeholders to push for policy change.

What makes this initiative so powerful is our ability to leverage the unique perspectives offered by our diverse student body and utilize the vast resources and research available at UC Berkeley. The unwavering support and encouragement from university faculty, including Professor Ferus-Comelo, catalyzed our endeavors, fostering an environment where innovation and compassion thrived. As we delved into the complexities of the labor rights landscape, we recognized the interconnectedness of social, economic, and environmental factors that impact vulnerable workers worldwide. Our collaborative efforts culminated in a list of action items aimed at ensuring that workers' rights are protected and that fairness prevails throughout the global supply chains. Not only did this experience empower us as change-makers, but it also demonstrated the indispensable role universities play in nurturing socially conscious individuals who actively engage with communities to bring about positive transformations for the greater good. By integrating academic excellence with practical application and community involvement, universities can be pivotal agents in driving social justice initiatives, fostering a generation of advocates committed to making the world a more equitable and just place for all.

To combat wage theft effectively, it is essential to develop a comprehensive definition of the phenomenon. By recognizing and addressing these different manifestations, efforts can be directed toward promoting fair labor practices and ensuring that workers receive their rightful wages. Wage theft is a form of labor exploitation that deprives workers of their rightful earnings. The impact of wage theft on garment workers is severe. Denied their rightful earnings, workers face economic hardship, leading to physical and mental health issues, limited access to education and essential services, and constant financial stress. This exploitation disproportionately affects low-wage workers, including women, people of color, and immigrant workers, who are more likely to hold low-wage jobs.

Major fashion brands play a significant role in perpetuating wage theft. These brands make unilateral decisions regarding production, taking advantage of the state's inability to enforce higher wages. Additionally, they fail to implement cost-sharing practices across the supply chain, burdening workers with the costs and consequences of cost-cutting measures. This imbalance of power enables brands to accumulate excessive wealth at the expense of the workers. The prevailing supply chain structure in the global garment industry is characterized by a small number of powerful brands that maintain control over numerous suppliers. These suppliers, often contracted manufacturers, engage in low-value manufacturing without significant opportunities for advancement. As a result, workers face limited prospects for skills development or upward mobility within the industry. This supply chain structure has several consequences that contribute to wage theft. Garment workers and suppliers are compelled to remain constantly available to meet the demands of global North producers, driven by fierce competition. Furthermore, the minimum wage set at the national level is often below the level required for workers to sustain a decent standard of living. This perpetuates poverty-level wages and exacerbates the vulnerability of workers, who often live from paycheck to paycheck.

A crucial opportunity for addressing wage theft lies in the establishment of unions for garment workers. Unions can advocate for progressively increasing wages to reach a living wage, ensuring fair compensation, and improving workers' livelihoods. Without such unions, workers inadvertently end up contributing to a situation where brands' profits are artificially increased while they continue to face exploitation. The concept of a living wage also emerges as a critical consideration. A living wage is an income necessary for workers and their families to afford a decent standard of living, encompassing essential needs such as food, housing, education, health care, transportation, clothing, and unexpected expenses. Upholding the principle of a living wage is a moral imperative and a fundamental human right, as recognized by the United Nations and the International Labour Organization (2021).

### *Unveiling the Future of Garment Workers and the Implications of COVID-19 on Wage Theft in the Global South*

The COVID-19 pandemic exacerbated the issue of wage theft in the global garment industry, leading to unprecedented levels of exploitation. With falling sales and store closures, many factories in the Global South were forced to shut down due to an overwhelming number of order cancellations and reduced demand for lower-priced garments. This mass closure of factories resulted in widespread dismissals of workers, further exacerbating their vulnerable situation.

Research conducted by the Worker Rights Consortium revealed that 31 export garment factories failed to pay their workers the legally earned severance. This equated to a loss of $39.8 million for 37,637 individuals within these 31 facilities alone. On average, this corresponds to approximately 5 months' rent in wages per garment worker (more than $1000/person). Major brands such as Adidas, Amazon, Nike, and Target were among those contracting from these factories, implicating their role in perpetuating wage theft and labor rights violations.

The power imbalance between fashion brands and suppliers became apparent during the pandemic when brands simply canceled orders, leaving suppliers and workers without income. Many working contracts in the industry were structured in a way that tied workers' pay to the output they produced. This piece-rate system made it easier for employers to manipulate wages and withhold payment. Additionally, the fact that brands do not directly own the factories (suppliers) where garment workers are employed allowed brands to distance themselves from any legal responsibilities towards the workers producing their clothes. The lack of accountability and regulation in this regard allows brands to engage in purchasing practices that undermine labor laws and workers' rights.

It is estimated that within the first 13 months of the pandemic, garment workers globally lost a staggering $11.85 billion in income. The lack of regulation in the industry enables brands and suppliers to prioritize cost-cutting measures, placing downward pressure on labor costs. This, in turn, leads suppliers to neglect their obligations, such as saving for future severance liabilities. The brands, as the financial beneficiaries, are responsible for ensuring that suppliers can adequately provide for their workers, especially in times of economic hardship.

Although the majority of brands in the garment industry, and subsequently their suppliers, formally commit to basic labor laws—including laws that ensure unemployment protections like worker severance—the lack of regulation allows them to utilize purchasing practices that put the implementation of these laws in jeopardy. The downward price pressure exerted on suppliers by brands incentivizes suppliers to minimize labor costs, which they are only able to do by neglecting perceptibly extraneous costs of labor like saving for future severance liabilities. As the brands are the supplier's financial beneficiaries, such savings are necessary to ensure factory owners meet their obligations and maintain a profit margin. Thus, decreasing the prevalence of labor rights abuse in the global apparel industry is contingent on the implementation of regulations that will effectively force brands to pay suppliers enough to make a profit and still be able to adequately provide for their workers in case economic relief becomes necessary.

### *Wage Theft in the Context of the Global Labor Migration Landscape*

In Bangladesh, the ready-made garment industry is a major employer, providing livelihoods for millions of people. However, it is disheartening to witness that these hardworking individuals are paid some of the lowest wages globally. These poverty-level wages stand in stark contrast to the prices consumers pay for clothing, and the prevailing piece-rate system further exacerbates the issue, leading to meager earnings for the workers. A worker producing garments for H&M in Cambodia shares this sentiment in an attempt to convey how vulnerable garment workers are due to the lack of a living wage, asserting to consumers that "[their] salary does not allow [them] to save money–it's barely enough to live." The Asian Floor Wage Alliance has proposed a living wage that takes into account factors like family size and basic needs, but the government's efforts to increase the minimum wage have not been enough. Brands must take responsibility and ensure fair wages for garment workers.

Large brands, at the top of the global supply chain, profit off of the cheap production of goods afforded to them by the wage theft business model. The lack of overarching jurisdiction over the global labor landscape that allows firms to take advantage of workers is a major barrier impeding migrant workers from being able to seek justice and reclaim their wages. Migrant workers, like most low-wage workers, are unlikely to file a claim, as they fear it will result in employer retaliation. It can also be very difficult, or even impossible, for them to file a claim without explicit evidence and/or in the case that the worker has already returned to their home country. In the case that the worker is able to obtain a successful ruling, there is a high probability that they will never receive their wages due to the minimal consequences noncompliance has on employers.

The COVID-19 pandemic amplified the inability of migrant workers to access wage justice, exposing key policy gaps and institutional inadequacy. As businesses were burdened with unforeseen financial pressures, millions of migrant workers (especially those on temporary contacts and those who are undocumented) were repatriated—sent back to their country of origin—without being paid their earned wages. Alternatively, a number of individuals were stranded in countries where they typically remain excluded from accessing social protection provisions, thus forcing them to accept poorer terms and conditions of employment (including reduced salaries), while others faced work permit termination and the possibility of deportation.

### *Conceptualizing Wage Theft to Strengthen Union Demands and Bargaining Power*

Addressing wage theft in the global garment industry requires collaborative efforts involving stakeholders such as universities, organizations like the AFWA, and policymakers. By fostering a comprehensive understanding of the problem, promoting fair labor practices, and advocating for policy changes, progress can be made toward combating wage theft and improving the lives of garment workers worldwide.

Major fashion brands have failed to ensure fair wages for garment workers, leaving them in severe poverty that often leads to physical and mental health issues, lack of access to education and services, and constant stress. Through the development of a comprehensive definition of wage theft, the primary goal of this collaborative study was to shed light on the systematic practices that result in garment workers being denied fair wages for their labor. Complex supply chains, price-based competition, reliance on low-cost labor, lack of transparency, and insufficient regulation are just some of the underlying factors contributing to wage theft. By examining these factors within the context of stakeholder partnerships and impact, it is clear that major fashion brands have failed to ensure a living wage for workers because there is nothing holding them responsible for doing so.

### *Insights and Strategies From the Global North: Lessons Learned for Addressing Wage Theft in the Garment Industry*

By exploring the concept of wage theft from a multitude of perspectives, extrapolating the key learnings from case studies, and assessing the impact of the COVID-19 crisis in both the Global North and Global South, we have been able to make a valuable comparison between the presence of wage theft in more developed countries and the rampant wage theft being experienced by garment workers in the Global South. Ultimately, we resolved that decreasing the prevalence of labor rights abuse in the global apparel industry is contingent on the implementation of regulations that will effectively force brands to pay suppliers enough to make a profit and still be able to adequately provide for their workers in the case economic relief becomes necessary.

Governments around the world must acknowledge that wage theft is systemic and accept their role in implementing regulation, particularly in regards to holding lead firms in supply chains accountable for the wage theft occurring lower down in the supply chain. Joint liability for wage nonpayment between firms and their suppliers will ensure that businesses are not able to turn a blind eye to the labor violations of their contractors, as it gives them no choice but to take on the burden of production oversight.

Improving the judicial process for wage claims must also become a priority for governments, as it is currently inaccessible to many workers and wholly ineffective in enforcing payment by firms. Investing in the development of technological systems to identify and relay evidence of wage theft—requiring employers to electronically track worker hours, provide workers with pay stubs, and then relay this information to the government—could also be a strong step in streamlining the judicial process. Furthermore, to ensure compliance of firms, governments must impose substantial penalties on businesses that ignore judgments on wages. This could include temporary license revocation, establishing a rapid accrual of noncompliance penalties, prohibiting the transportation of goods across internal and international borders, and/or giving workers access to commercial assets to fulfill wage claims until wages are paid. Lastly, looking at solutions utilized in the global North, it may be valuable for the AFWA to advocate for the creation of a global severance fund to provide workers with a safety net in the case that their factory is unable to provide severance.

On a high level, U.S. solutions to wage theft consist of increasing funding for enforcement agencies, developing better enforcement strategies, implementing significant civil monetary penalties (CMPs) to deter violations, and introducing labor law reform. Examples of California law reform include the SB 62 Act and Assembly Bill 1003. The Garment Worker Protection Act (SB 62 Act), signed into law by Governor Newsom, makes California the first state to require hourly wages for garment workers. This bill serves to promote brand accountability, prohibits piece-work (a practice allowing for manufacturers to pay their workers per garment, resulting in salaries lower than $6/hr), and penalizes both brands and their suppliers for instances of wage theft (Dir, 2022; Solá-Santiago, 2022). Effective January 1, 2022, Assemblywoman Lorena Gonzalez's Assembly Bill 1003 establishes that the intentional theft of wages or tips by employers of an amount greater than $950 for one employee, or $2,350 for two or more employees, is punishable as grand theft (Sanderson, 2021).

### *AFWA Opportunities for Growth: Advocating for the Implementation of New Strategies to Reduce Labor Violations in the Global Garment Industry*

In today's interconnected world of global business, the absence of a centralized authority poses significant challenges when it comes to regulating supply chains and eliminating worker exploitation. With no overarching entity responsible for global labor market oversight, the burden falls on individual governments to enforce regulations within the countries where business operations are conducted. This section explores the importance of government intervention on a global scale and proposes strategies to address systemic issues, including wage theft and poor working conditions.

The tragic collapse of the Rana Plaza factory in Bangladesh in 2013, which claimed the lives of over a thousand workers, served as a catalyst for the establishment of initiatives like the *Accord on Fire and Building Safety* and the *Alliance for Bangladesh Worker Safety*. These initiatives aimed to enhance workplace safety, improve working conditions, and hold brands accountable for worker safety through rigorous inspections, remediation, training, and complaint resolution. Moreover, organizations such as the AFWA and the Fair Wear Foundation have also undertaken efforts to address living wages, with the Wage Forward Campaign advocating for a living wage in the garment industry through stakeholder collaboration.

Despite these commendable initiatives, progress in improving working conditions and ensuring fair wages in the garment industry has been limited. While some brands have made efforts to address poor working conditions and commit to a fair living wage roadmap, overall implementation remains inadequate. For instance, H&M's failure to fulfill its promises highlights the challenges in achieving a living wage for garment workers in Bangladesh and beyond, and no worker in Bangladesh receives a living wage. Various government interventions, such as the Joint Employer Liability Legal Strategy, SB 62 Act, and EU legislation on Living Wage, have also fallen short in providing adequate wages for garment workers (Clean Clothes Campaign, n.d.; Farrell, 2013; Mirdha, 2016; Musiolek, 2018).

Resolving the complex issue of low wages in the garment industry, especially in Bangladesh, requires a comprehensive approach that surpasses existing initiatives. Increasing awareness, implementing NGO initiatives, and enacting government legislation on a global scale are essential components of a viable solution. Building on the success of the Accord on Fire and Building Safety, the establishment of a living wage accord could serve as a binding agreement between apparel brands, factories, and trade unions. Regular audits would ensure adherence to living wage standards, while government regulations could set minimum wage levels and impose significant taxes on noncompliant companies. Factories violating wage laws could face fines or closures. By addressing these systemic challenges and enacting robust and collaborative measures, we can pave the way towards a more equitable and just future for garment workers worldwide.

### *Shifting the Narrative and Messaging Strategy*

Unlike the practices in the United States, the AFWA faces challenges in promptly enforcing new rules through national institutions. Moreover, the producing countries under the AFWA's mission cannot afford the luxury U.S. brands enjoy in outsourcing wages from their home country abroad. Therefore, a strategic approach involves calling out fashion brands on the playing field, targeting their professional working prestige. By running campaigns that shed light on poor management practices and flawed decision-making and illustrating the potential for increased profitability, the AFWA can speak in the language that resonates with the brands and their competitors. For instance, the AFWA can highlight the inefficiencies in their supply chains, the lack of employee investment, and the detrimental impact on profits and market share resulting from spontaneous and ill-informed decisions. This tactic exerts pressure on brands and associated suppliers within the professional business landscape, urging them to take action.

### *Building Partnerships*

While the AFWA plays a pivotal role in addressing labor injustices, it is essential to recognize that several other organizations are also dedicated to achieving this shared goal. One such organization is the Clean Clothes Campaign, a research and advocacy group focused on empowering workers, providing invaluable resources and support to numerous organizations actively tackling labor issues. Additionally, the Global Living Wage Coalition (GLWC) aligns its mission with the AFWA, striving to promote living wages and offering the potential for a valuable partnership in future campaigns. To achieve fair compensation for workers, the GLWC adopts Anker's methodology, which has been successfully employed by Patagonia's board, providing a robust framework for advocating fair pay (Global Living Wage Coalition, 2022).

Recognizing and collaborating with these organizations could enhance the impact of the AFWA's efforts and contribute to a broader, collective push for improved labor conditions worldwide. By joining forces with the Clean Clothes Campaign, the AFWA could gain access to a wealth of knowledge and expertise in worker-oriented initiatives, fostering a more comprehensive approach to labor rights advocacy. Similarly, partnering with the GLWC could strengthen the AFWA's campaigns by incorporating data-driven methodologies to determine living wages, bolstering their position in advocating for fair wages and better working conditions in the fashion industry. As the AFWA continues its mission to create a more equitable and just labor environment, these strategic collaborations with like-minded organizations can prove instrumental in driving meaningful change. By leveraging the experiences and expertise of the Clean Clothes Campaign and the GLWC, the AFWA can further solidify its impact, leaving a lasting and positive legacy in pursuing fair treatment and improved livelihoods for garment workers worldwide.

### *Advocate for the Creation of a Global Severance Fund*

To address the pressing challenges posed by wage theft in the global labor landscape, the AFWA can significantly contribute by advocating for the establishment of a robust and transformative global severance fund, such as the "Fired then Robbed" initiative. This innovative fund, backed by labor unions and dedicated advocacy groups worldwide, would serve as a vital safety net for workers who find themselves in dire circumstances when their factories fail to provide them with the rightful severance they deserve. This initiative's sustainability would be ensured through compulsory contributions from endorsing brands and retailers, thereby cementing a collective responsibility to protect workers' rights. In cases where a factory associated with a signatory company neglects to fulfill its obligation of providing severance, the fund would act swiftly, stepping in to safeguard the well-being of affected workers and extending the much-needed support they deserve. By forging partnerships and collaborations with like-minded organizations committed to improving global labor conditions, the AFWA can elevate its efforts and amplify awareness about these critical issues, making strides towards a fairer and more just work environment for workers across the globe.

### *Harnessing Technology and Stakeholder Collaboration*

Blockchain is a decentralized system that enables secure, peer-to-peer transactions without the need for a third-party intermediary (Nakamoto, n.d.). It utilizes cryptographic proof to ensure transparency, immutability, and verification of assets and transactions, making it an innovative and efficient technology for various industries (Chen et al., 2018). Blockchain technology holds significant potential to enhance transparency and traceability within the garment industry. It enables the tracking of garment origins, workers' wages, and shipping information, empowering consumers to make informed choices and hold brands accountable for fair labor practices. By exclusively supporting brands committed to fair labor practices, consumer pressure can incentivize other brands to follow suit. NGOs, labor rights groups, and unions also play a crucial role in advocating for living wages through campaigns and supporting workers' rights.

Levi Strauss & Co. is one compelling case study for implementing blockchain technology. Through their adoption of blockchain, the company has improved supply chain management, fostered sustainable practices, and amplified worker voices. They have employed a blockchain-based survey platform to gather data from workers, leading to improved working conditions and reduced absenteeism. Levi Strauss & Co.'s utilization of blockchain has increased transparency, enabled real-time monitoring of supplier progress, and enhanced the overall worker experience within supply chains. This example exemplifies the potential of blockchain to enhance ethical practices and improve the worker experience within supply chains.

While no single solution can completely solve the challenges garment workers face, a combination of approaches holds great potential for significantly improving their lives. By leveraging blockchain technology, advocating for fair wages, exerting consumer pressure, and implementing government interventions on a global scale, alongside stakeholder collaboration, robust regulation, and technological advancements, positive changes can be made to the industry and the experiences of those working within it. This collective effort strives to create a future where exploitation is eradicated and every worker receives the dignity and compensation they deserve, establishing a sustainable path towards fair wages and improved worker well-being.

***Future Pathways of Exploration: Implications for the Authors' Understanding of Justice***

*Zenia's Perspective: Learning to Engage in Advocacy From Diverse Fields*

Pursuing a minor in public policy has further nurtured my interest in this field and deepened my understanding of its profound impact on community health outcomes. Hence, when the opportunity arose to choose an organization to collaborate with, the AFWA immediately captured my attention. Their vital work in combating the health disparities, magnified by the COVID-19 pandemic, in the global South resulting from wage theft resonated deeply with me. Although this aspect was not the central objective of our project, it provided me with an opportunity to closely examine the underlying factors contributing to wage theft and the dire consequences, particularly extreme poverty, experienced by individuals in the global south. These circumstances often result in unfavorable health conditions, further emphasizing the urgency for change.

Through this project, I gained a more comprehensive understanding of issues beyond my STEM-focused education, expanding the depth of my knowledge base. It has ignited a genuine passion for policy research within me, setting the stage for my future aspirations. As I pursue a career in medicine, I aim to combine my expertise in health care with my growing interest in policy. My ultimate goal is to contribute to the field of public health and actively work towards policy changes that improve and standardize healthcare quality worldwide.

Moreover, this project sparked a desire within me to establish more profound, lasting connections within my native countries, Pakistan and Bangladesh. I am determined to promote upward mobility, particularly for women who face limited rights and opportunities within these patriarchal societies. My commitment to effecting positive change in these regions has become an integral part of my long-term vision and I hope to one day establish a nonprofit that will increase access to technical and vocational training for Women in Bangladesh.

Working collaboratively with the AFWA has significantly heightened my awareness of the unethical labor practices prevalent in the fast fashion industry. Recognizing that consumer demand drives these brands, I have taken a firm stand by completely boycotting companies such as Forever 21 and Shein. Instead, I have actively shifted my shopping preferences towards supporting small businesses and exploring secondhand shops, aligning my actions with my values. By committing to this decision to shop sustainably, although it may cost more at times, I believe that I am setting an example for those in my inner circle, which could influence them to do the same—and, at the very least, bring some visibility to the issue of fast fashion.

*Alexis's Perspective*

Working with AFWA has been a transformative experience that has deeply influenced my perspective on justice in the global supply chain, specifically within the fashion industry. Through this project, I have learned about the significance of equal human rights and fashion brands' responsibility to ensure a living wage for their workers. This newfound understanding has expanded my knowledge and motivated me to take concrete actions in my academic and personal life to address the prevalent labor rights issues in this industry. My time with AFWA has shaped my outlook on justice and inspired me to pursue further exploration and advocacy in the fashion industry's future pathways.

Motivated by my participation in AFWA, I enrolled in a global supply chain class that specifically emphasized the garment industry. During the course, I actively contributed to a group project investigating living wages in the global garment industry, providing valuable insights into labor rights challenges workers face. In this insightful class, I proposed two solutions to address the wage issue in Bangladesh's garment industry: the Living Wage Accord and the PermaWage app. The Accord, if adopted, proposes a binding agreement for fair pay, transparency, and oversight, while the PermaWage app seeks to empower workers, rectify wage disparities, and ensure transparency and fairness while protecting workers' rights.

During my association with AFWA, I acquired pivotal insights into sustainable fashion and ethical labor practices, deeply influencing my academic endeavors throughout college. This profound understanding, rooted in hands-on experience, became a primary topic of my senior research thesis, where I explored feasible solutions and technological interventions within the fashion domain. Specifically, I focused on utilizing blockchain technology (BT) in the fashion industry and investigated its potential to tackle the aforementioned issue. Integrating BT in the fashion industry promotes justice and fair compensation for garment workers. By utilizing BT, brands can track the entire supply chain, including the fabric's origin, the workers of garments, the wages they receive, and the shipment details. This transparency empowers consumers to trace the supply chain of their clothes, verify that workers were paid a living wage, and make more informed choices. Furthermore, it incentivizes brands and retailers to pay fair wages to avoid negative publicity and holds them accountable for ensuring ethical treatment of workers.

Extending far beyond academia, my transformative experiences with AFWA have been foundational in shaping the ethos and entrepreneurial decisions of CINC COLLECTIVE LLC, my sustainable fashion brand. The insights garnered from this partnership illuminated the systemic challenges within the fashion industry, deepening my dedication and reinforcing my commitment to implementing responsible manufacturing, ethical sourcing, and sustainable practices throughout CINC COLLECTIVE's supply chain. As the brand has evolved, AFWA's influence is evident in our ethos, a beacon of change that emphasizes circular fashion, sustainability, and fair labor practices. My unwavering commitment drives me to democratize sustainable fashion, educating consumers and inspiring other brands to champion these core values in their operations. The journey with AFWA has been instrumental in guiding my academic and entrepreneurial endeavors, catalyzing a broader movement in the fashion industry toward responsibility, sustainability, transparency, and equity while creating a lasting impact on the community. Through education, action, and relentless dedication, I aim to foster a transformative path forward in fashion, ensuring that it uplifts rather than exploits.

Recently, I had the privilege of being approached by Rowaiye, the founder of the Larry Rowbs Foundation, with an extraordinary opportunity to serve as a board member for their organization. This foundation is dedicated to promoting innovation and sustainability in Africa's textile industry through recycling initiatives, which perfectly aligns with my commitment to ethical practices in fashion. Their vision involves creating a circular economy by establishing a clothing recycling facility and utilizing the proceeds to launch a recycling and fashion school. With members from 14 countries, the foundation seeks individuals like me to raise awareness, collaborate, and drive transformative change for a sustainable future, offering opportunities for global impact, exposure to influential organizations, and career advancement.

My journey in exploring pathways of justice in the fashion industry through my involvement with AFWA, academic pursuits, founding CINC COLLECTIVE LLC, and collaborating with the Larry Rowbs Foundation has been enlightening and empowering. My experiences have deepened my understanding of labor rights complexities and sustainable fashion practices, fueling my passion for equal human rights and labor practices. This motivation drives me to engage in projects for positive change, as I believe every action contributes to a more equitable world. I'm committed to advocating for justice, transparency, and worker empowerment in the fashion industry, emphasizing ethics and fairness. Partnering with AFWA not only enriched my knowledge but inspired me to actively contribute to their mission and further immerse myself in sustainable practices, instilling a passion for ethical fashion.

## *Conclusion*

Our partnership with the AFWA has been a transformative journey for us as students and as advocates for workers' rights. As we embarked on this journey, we aimed to develop a comprehensive concept of wage theft and draw insights from successful campaigns and lawsuits in the United States. These efforts provided invaluable knowledge to bolster the fight against wage theft, striving for a just future of work in the global fashion industry. Together with the AFWA, we demonstrated a shared commitment to driving systemic change and promoting fair conditions for garment workers across global supply chains. Central to our collaborative effort was the development of educational pamphlets. These were not just materials, but tools of awareness that we strategically distributed to students, professionals, and everyday consumers. By reaching this diverse audience, we aimed to increase awareness of the issues at hand and inspire policy change by engaging key stakeholders in the fashion industry. Continuously supporting and fostering initiatives like this is essential to address labor rights issues and foster a more equitable and just environment for all workers within the global fashion industry.

It is clear that urgent action is needed to combat wage theft and promote social justice in the global fashion industry. We must recognize the responsibility we have as consumers, activists, policymakers, and members of society to demand change and support initiatives that uphold the rights and well-being of garment workers. By raising awareness, supporting ethical brands, advocating for legislative changes, empowering workers via trade unions and worker-led movements, and fostering collaboration and knowledge sharing between research institutions and labor organizations, the choices of consumers and advocates have the power to shape the future of the garment industry.

## References

Chen, G., Xu, B., Lu, M., & Chen, N.-S. (2018). Exploring blockchain technology and its potential applications for education. *Smart Learning Environments, 5*(1), 1. https://doi.org/10.1186/s40561-017-0050-x

Clean Clothes Campaign. (2021, July). Workers owed $11.85 billion after fashion brands' inaction. https://cleanclothes.org/news/2021/workers-owed-1185-billion-after-fashion-brands-inaction

Clean Clothes Campaign. (2023, May). Pay your workers. https://cleanclothes.org/campaigns/pay-your-workers

Dir. (2022). *Garment Worker Protection Act frequently asked questions.* https://www.dir.ca.gov/dlse/GarmentFAQs/

Farrell, S. (2013, November 25). H&M pledges living wage for textile workers in Bangladesh and Cambodia. *The Guardian*, Guardian News and Media. https://www.theguardian.com/business/2013/nov/25/h-m-living-wage-textile-workers-bangladesh-cambodia

Global Living Wage Coalition. (2022, April). *The Anker methodology for estimating a living wage.* https://www.globallivingwage.org/about/anker-methodology/#:~:text=The%20living%20wage%20methodology%20has,is%20being%20paid%20to%20workers

International Labour Organization. (2021). World Social Protection Report 2020-22. https://www.ilo.org/wcmsp5/groups/public/@ed_protect/@soc_sec/documents/publication/wcms_817572.pdf

Levin, M. B., Bowie, J. V., Ragsdale, S. K., Gawad, A. L., Cooper, L. A., & Sharfstein, J. M. (2021). Enhancing community engagement by schools and programs of Public Health in the United States. *Annual Review of Public Health, 42*(1), 405–421. https://doi.org/10.1146/annurev-publhealth-090419-102324

Mirdha, R. U. (2016, March 9). H&M to buy more garment items from Bangladesh: Official. *The Daily Star.* www.thedailystar.net/business/hm-buy-more-garment-items-bangladesh-official-788515

Musiolek, B. (2018, September). H&M: Fair living wages were promised, poverty wages are the reality. *Turn Around H&M*, Clean Clothes Campaign. turnaroundhm.org/

Nakamoto, S. (n.d.). Bitcoin: A peer-to-peer electronic cash system. https://bitcoin.org/bitcoin.pdf*Labor Justice*. globallaborjustice.org/portfolio_page/hm-and-gap-report-press-release/

Sanderson, S. (2021, November 24). California employers: Review your wage and hour policies for state compliance. *MNK Law*. https://mnklawyers.com/california-employers-review-your-wage-and-hour-policies-for-state-compliance/

Solá-Santiago, F. (2022, January 17). For activists, the Garment Worker Protection Act is just the beginning. What California SB 62 Act means for garment workers. https://www.refinery29.com/en-us/2022/01/10832734/garment-workers-protection-act-explained

Chapter 4

# The Future of Work/ers Through the Pandemic Portal—An Organizer's Perspective

*Taylor Valci*

Peering at the dismayed faces of my colleagues, I felt truly helpless. The year was 2020, and at the time I lacked all knowledge of the framework and articulation surrounding unions; yet, the weight of the managerial neglect and abuse I experienced was unmistakable. In the height of the COVID-19 pandemic, City Net Homeless Services hired dozens of "temporary employees" after the Orange County Board of Supervisors granted them a contract to be the primary facilitators of California's Project Room Key, the initiative to use vacant hotels as shelters for unhoused communities. Initially, I was elated to be hired after losing my previous job during the pandemic's outbreak, but it did not take long for the truth of the word "temporary" to reveal itself. My entire team was hired under these pretenses: a loophole in the labor system that allowed our employers to deny us health insurance, pay us minimum wage, demand endless hours of work, and receive no protection or guarantee of future employment. For a year, my colleagues and I lived in fear of the impending decision from the Orange County Board of Supervisors to end our program. We constantly were asked to perform tasks outside of our job descriptions, including intense manual labor along with cleaning and disposing of hazardous materials without protection or training. We witnessed death after death after death of folks placed in those hotels, with no acknowledgment, space, or professional support provided for the grief we experienced. The daily reminders of our country's failing housing system loomed large, but the greatest failure I experienced was the neglect and abuse from my employer. I will never forget the day when we all sat in a conference room and mourned over the state of our employment, feeling utterly hopeless. How I wish I knew what it meant to unionize at that time. How I wish I knew there were avenues in our labor system that could have protected us. How I wish I knew then what I know now.

The events that transpired during my time at City Net Homeless Services inspired me to return to school and finish my bachelor's degree, specifically with the goal of widening my understanding of labor in America. I did not have the language or knowledge to fight against the abuses of my employer at the time, but I knew what was happening was wrong, and I desperately desired to gain ample comprehension of how such exploitation could be prevented in the future. For this reason, I enrolled in Dr. Anibel Ferus-Comelo's course, Work, Justice, and the Labor Movement, during my first semester at UC Berkeley. This class revolutionized my understanding of labor in America. The first half of the semester was dedicated to developing an acute awareness of both past and present labor struggles in America and abroad, with topics explored such as surveillance in the workplace, LGBTQ+ rights, racial disparity and oppression, immigrant experiences, and workplace hazards, accompanied by historical studies of the 1981 PATCO strike, the Wagner and Taft-Hartley Acts, and more. I was dumbfounded by how much of this information was absent from my K-12 education, and yet, after observing the value capitalism places on productivity over a healthy and happy human existence, the calculation of refraining from educating children on labor history became perfectly clear.

One of the most incredible aspects of Dr. Ferus-Comelo's approach to university education is her dedication to involving her students in current labor activism and organization. I had the opportunity to meet representatives from the California Domestic Workers Coalition (CDWC) who expressed a need to gather information and collect researched reports on the quantity, intensity, and geography of workplace violations. This was my first time ever interacting with a union, and I was amazed by the level of dedication displayed in their efforts to prevent workplace violations. In the course of the project, colleagues and I collected over 400 surveys of represented workers through phone calls conducted in four different languages. My interactions with these members spanned a broad expanse, including some who were not interested in sharing their experiences at all and others who were eager for someone to listen to their stories of labor violations as a domestic worker. What I saw through this project was the power of hope in a union. Many workers did not want to answer the 20-minute survey as they did not believe such time would actually contribute to their benefit, and sadly, this is reasonable. In this course, I learned about the scores of ways unions and organizing efforts have been viciously thwarted by those with immense power under capitalism, and I could hear this very exhaustion and despair from the voices of those I spoke with during the time of this project. Conversely, there are still many who fiercely hope for a more equitable future. Many workers were elated to receive a call from someone who was interested in their daily struggles and wanted to play a role in implementing a tangible solution. I've come to find in the time that has passed since this project that this wide spectrum of hope is typical in union organizing, and it is the insurmountable task of every organizer to bolster hope under a capitalist system that actively works to squash all ambition of a truly equitable world.

After collecting this information from the CDWC members, we transformed it into valuable deliverables including collections of maps and statistics, as well as social media campaigns that we presented to the representatives at the California Domestic Workers Coalition. This was the first time in my academic career in which I felt my work as an undergraduate student directly impacted real people in my community. I learned that there is incredible power in unionizing but also that there are hostile systems actively working to dismantle the efforts of collective action. The labor movement, its history, its struggles, and its dreams were all made known to me in this course, and I became resolved in my dedication to its success.

The following semester, after experiencing such life-changing growth in her fall course, I chose to take another of Dr. Ferus-Comelo's courses, this one titled Collaborative Innovation. This course intersected the fields of business, theater, and public policy, requiring students to work across sectors and innovate solutions to some of the world's biggest problems. I was most impacted by this class through the final project, in which we worked in groups on research projects assigned to us by designated community partners. Due to my occupational history working within the health care system to assist those in the unhoused community with receiving federal and state disability benefits, I requested to be placed with SEIU 2015, which represents long-term caregivers in California. The policy leaders at this organization met with my team and me to discuss their need to explore multiple funding options for a long-term health care solution in

California. In the process of accomplishing this, my team and I had the unique opportunity of meeting with several experts in this field, including those directly involved in long-term care policy work in the California State Assembly and Senate. This experience proved pivotal in sparking a deep interest within myself for both labor-related and health care–related policies, specifically at the state level. While I did not interact with any SEIU 2015 members during this project, the knowledge I gained through the expertise of incredibly passionate and labor-minded professionals was exceptional. At the end of the semester, we presented four possible frameworks to the policy leaders at SEIU 2015. The first of these was social insurance, which is a model largely used in Europe. This encompasses a combination of funding sources, including employee and employer payroll taxes, and covers all contributors, regardless of income. The second was to borrow the model from the Washington State Cares Act, which is funded by a 0.58% employee payroll tax but does not cover the entire population. We also discussed the expansion of Medi-Cal by increasing the maximum income requirements to $30,000. To pay for this would require a drastic reallocation of the California General Fund, but it would target providing long-term care to those who most need it. Finally, we decided to think radically about solutions that aren't seen around the world right now, such as a wealth or corporate tax. Here in California, an increase of just 1% in the corporate tax would raise $17.5 billion, more than covering the cost of long-term care. We presented these solutions to the policy leaders at SEIU 2015, and this provided significant assistance in the policy proposals they are currently drafting. Again, unlike any other class I have ever taken at the undergraduate level, Collaborative Innovation facilitated community interactions that deeply impacted me. The class widened my understanding of the importance of policy in labor advocacy and the necessity to fight for radical change in all levels of political action.

Because of the magnitude of importance my interactions with these labor unions held in my life, I decided to apply for the UC Berkeley Labor Center's Labor Summer Program, in which I was paired with Teamsters 2010 as an organizing intern. I spent the summer speaking to clerical workers at UC Berkeley, discussing their wages, benefits, complaints, fears, and hopes. We fought against the UC Administration's efforts to prolong contract agreements and minimize the offers presented to their employees. Through this experience, I witnessed the many ways in which the UC system exploits its employees and the strong efforts of those workers to fight against it. Many times throughout my journey of understanding capitalism, I have felt overwhelmed and dismayed by the sheer size and power of the institutions that work so fervently against the struggle for worker's rights. Yet, in standing with Teamsters 2010, I felt emboldened to believe in a world in which workers can stand up to these major forces. Still, it was not all victories. My time as an organizer for Teamsters 2010 revealed the immense fatigue felt by workers who genuinely hope for a fairer working experience but are consistently blockaded by the enormity of resources and power held by their employers. This experience fostered both intimidation and inspiration within me, but more importantly, determination.

There are as many ways to be called into the labor movement as there are laborers in this world. For me, however, this calling manifested from my time as an undergraduate university student. The paradox is not lost on me that it was at a major institution that habitually fails its employees in which I was able to experience the greatest growth of fervor in my personal labor movement story. Just recently, 48,000 graduate students across all of the UC schools were forced to go on strike after their demands were repeatedly ignored throughout contract negotiations, a testament to the dissonance of the UC system's ability to bolster the voices of real change-makers like Dr. Ferus-Comelo while still failing to provide for the basic needs of their workers. My story is meant to reflect the voices of resistance within the university setting that seek to develop true labor equity in all levels of employment. Dr. Anibel Ferus-Comelo is truly a shining light on the UC Berkeley campus, always aware of exploitation enacted by her own employer, and always willing to teach about and fight alongside those standing in resistance. The UC Berkeley Labor Center similarly cultivates strength and resilience amongst students and university employees alike, as it has done in me. While the university system as a whole looms large in my mind as a corporatization of what should be shared knowledge, I have been so incredibly emboldened by those who share their passions and endeavors in the dismantling of this system. Furthermore, Professor Ferus-Comelo and the UC Berkeley Labor Center organized and established tangible connections between myself and my community, an effort that is hardly seen in typical university settings. The result of all these factors within me is hope.

Three years ago, I did not know that I could work to form a union amongst my peers. I did not know the ways in which I could fight for our protection and well-being. I did not understand collective action and the power of masses. But I do now. My time at City Net Homeless Services was characterized by hopelessness, like there was no possible way to change the realities of my working situation. But after my time working with the California Domestic Workers Coalition, SEIU 2015, and Teamsters 2010, I am now filled with determination and hope. I see myself as an integral part of the inevitable great worker's revolution to come, and I am so deeply resolved in dedicating my efforts to this dream. But in the meantime, I feel hope in the present. What I experienced at City Net Homeless Services will never happen again, for even though I might be employed under abusive bosses or hostile work environments, I know my power as a worker now, and that changes everything. I know that I can stand up and unite with my peers. In every space in which my labor is sold, I will fight for my dignity and equity as well as those working with me. There is a future in which the laborers of this world shall no longer endure the brutal exploitation that capitalism demands. I have been radicalized and enlivened to pursue this reality, and it is through both the failings of the California university system to provide equitable treatment to their employees as well as its success in bolstering voices and spaces of revolutionary change in which my personal transformation has occurred.

## Suggested Reading

Cohen, M., Tell, E., & Albright, B. (2020). Learning from new state initiatives in financing long-term services and supports. *Innovation in Aging*, 4(1), 717. https://doi.org/10.1093/geroni/igaa057.2530

Kaplan, J. (2021). Why aren't large corporations paying their fair share of taxes? California Budget and Policy Center. https://calbudgetcenter.org/resources/why-arent-large-corporations-paying-their-fair-share-of-taxes/

Staff. (2022, January 10). Read our full coverage of the UC academic workers' strike. *Los Angeles Times*. https://www.latimes.com/california/story/2022-11-30/read-our-full-coverage-of-the-uc-strike-of-48-000-academic-workers

Streett, L. (2001). *Understanding Medi-Cal: Long-Term Care*. Medi-Cal Policy Institute.

# Section II

# Community Based Research as Social Justice

**Chapter 5**

# Embodying Equity Through Engaged Research: A View From Within Philanthropic Initiatives for Social Change

*Angela K. Frusciante*

> *Meaning making is the heart of human creative agency; Shared meaning making is the soul of change efforts that move toward greater equity; Knowledge work embraces both.*

Knowledge work, as the embodied practice of engaged scholars, is becoming an identifiable aspect of social change strategies and philanthropically funded change initiatives. Although learning, capacity building, and evaluation have already taken hold within the philanthropic sector, "knowledge work," defined in the context of equity intentions, complex systems, and desires for deeper and broader inclusion of lived experience, is still emerging as an essential function. However, knowledge work is now poised to become a subfield within philanthropy. Embracing the ideas and practices of engaged research as the core of knowledge work is crucial in social change initiatives because these efforts require flexibility and collaboration in aligning methodologies with the values and rhythms of social change processes. In this chapter, I assert that the essence of knowledge work, regardless of methodology or methods, is shared meaning making. I discuss knowledge work from inside philanthropically funded efforts toward social change. I enter in through a belief that these initiatives, even with their inherent power differentials, have the possibility to provide intentional space for agency and social creativity.

In the first part, I outline the conceptual areas that ground knowledge work in the sector: social change, philanthropic strategy, knowledge construction, and frameworks for meaning making. In the second part of the chapter, I describe methodological decisions made in three case examples that serve to highlight engaged research processes and to surface key insights about how knowledge work is taking hold in and through philanthropy.

I link parts one and two by locating myself through my lived experience and social change commitments and share a process I call "knowledge opportunity scanning" that guides my engaged research. Throughout, I emphasize how knowledge construction is equity work and how building this field from our practice is the grounding necessary to be true to the co-creative values of equitable social change.

## Philanthropy and the Social Sector in Context

To understand the importance of knowledge work within philanthropically funded initiatives, we need only to reflect on the perceived divisiveness of our times where competing narratives go even deeper than political partisanship. These narratives emerge from divergent views of the world, its structures, its issues and their causes, and ultimately vastly widening stances on the appropriate processes toward progress.

There is general awareness that the last decade has seen widespread challenges. Persistent inequities and inequitable life outcomes across various groups, increasing hate crimes, inter- and intranational conflict, climate crises, serious challenges to public education, health system failures revealed by a global pandemic, and the many persistent isms—sexism, racism, classism, ageism. Each raises questions about how current stressors affect democracy, how to re-energize our collective ability to address contemporary problems, and how we can embrace a diversity ideal that does not degrade into extreme divides.

For democratic society to work, it is essential for citizens to be understood as co-creators "reconstructing the world" (Boyte, 2011). Extreme divides spark fear that the civic engagement, social relationships, and shared problem-solving necessary for democracy are declining and that democracy can no longer be effective in meeting challenges, threats, and both human needs and aspirations.

Over the same decade, there has been a rise in the formalized social sector implemented through nonprofit organizations and codified by a tax code that encourages private investment in social action (Andrews, 1961; Berry, 2005). The social sector is the space for civic participation, community, advocacy, and societal exploration and innovation. Nonprofits participate in various ways in this space including as a mechanism of civic participation (Kluver, 2004).

Organized philanthropy is one aspect of the nonprofit sector that has grown in modern times (Anheier & Leat, 2013; Hall, 2006) and that increasingly influences the social space or public sphere (Karl & Katz, 1981; Lenkowsky, 2007; Thomson, 2022). Philanthropy has seen a vast expansion in the United States, reaching $485.85 billion in 2021 (Giving-USA, 2022).

Because of the power of its capital endowments, its institutionalization through foundation structures, and its separation from many public and market forces, philanthropy is increasingly called on, as itself a sector, to infuse the social space with not just funds, but also with energy, information, and strategic partnership to encourage civic activity and social change (Auspos et al., 2009; Ferris, 2017; Karlström et al., 2009).

As public or civic space decreases and private investment and big wealth increase, the social sector is becoming more formalized and depends on increasing amounts of private funding for perceived public good. Some call this infusion of private wealth into the social space, especially as it occurs through large foundations, "philanthrocapitalism" or "marketization" (Bishop, 2013; Eikenberry & Kluver, 2004), and offer questions and critique about philanthropy's influence in the civic arena (Barkan, 2013; Bartley, 2007; Brody & Tyler (2012); Ealy & Ealy, 2006; Eikenberry, 2006; Francis, 2019; Pevnick, 2013) and if or how philanthropy should be addressing structural inequities in society and even inside philanthropy itself (Arno et al., 2012; Cunningham et al., 2014; Redwood & King, 2014; Young et al., 2017).

With growth, the philanthropic sector is becoming increasingly formalized and professionalized. There are now university degree programs dedicated to it, consulting and training firms focused on it, and think tanks funded to explore it. As of 2009, there is a peer-reviewed journal (*The Foundation Review*) focused entirely on philanthropic research and practice. Although philanthropy has long been involved in funding external research, there is now a growing amount of research about philanthropy, often coming from inside philanthropy itself. This formalization of philanthropy has led to an almost obsession with traditional notions of strategic planning, data-based decision-making, and outcome-focused evaluative research (Brest, 2005, 2012; Coffman et al., 2013; Gugerty & Karlan, 2018; Kinarsky & Christie, 2022; Patrizi, 2006).

This formalization limits social change. This happens when requirements and practices reduce opportunities for people to come to shared values and framings for change. It happens when formalization does not hold space for people to show up as complex and in the wholeness of their lived experience. It happens when the incorporation of research processes re-create structures of dominance (Choudry, 2009a, 2009b; Fisher, 1983) rather than activating the shared meaning making essential to democracy and social change. Even as innovation is occurring in foundation structures and approach (Hagerty, 2012), the importance of knowledge construction practices is often overlooked or research methods used to exercise control over change efforts rather than to enable them (Frusciante, 2004).

I worry that reliance on private wealth in social space weakens society by reducing the sense that we are all equally in it together. I wonder how knowledge work can reclaim, within philanthropic initiatives, equity and social change goals that affirm human creative agency and responsibility for co-creating our world. I believe that embracing engaged research as a core philosophy and practice is one key approach that foundations can embody to buffer against these tendencies.

## Engaged Research as Equitable Social Change

Engaged research is a promising approach that breaks through these challenges by grounding methodology in a holistic understanding of social change and embracing lived experience. Engaged researchers center knowledge construction as active and embodied. Engaged research is designed as participatory, unapologetically equity-focused, action-oriented, and targeted to cause-based and social justice efforts (Bell, 2016; Schensul, 2010; Udani & Dobbs, 2021; Van Zandt et al., 2022; Wallerstein, 2021). Engaged research can provide space for reflection, inclusion, and shared power amongst all who participate, transparently addressing the ethical and logistical challenges this participation entails

(Reyna et al., 2021). Through engaged research as a practice of knowledge construction, participants can show up in holism and realize the creative agency necessary for equitable change and social justice.

At its core, engaged research has four elements that align it with social justice tenets:

> Reflexivity—those involved in the research are expected to be mindful of their own entry points, biases, privilege, and how they show up in various power structures.
>
> Partnership—with individuals, who are not from formal academic or research structures, as full participants in knowledge construction.
>
> Transparency—about the methodologies brought in or co-created through participation.
>
> Intentionality—of focus on real-time needs specific to groups and communities not traditionally prioritized in the mainstream distribution of private resources, public services, or political representation.

The focus on commitment, trust, and relationship make engaged research design incredibly innovative and rigorous. These values are important to both institutionalized research endeavors and progressive community change efforts.

## *Part I: Exploring Conceptual Areas*

Knowledge work, in philanthropically funded change initiatives relies on multiple lenses—views of social change, ideas about philanthropic strategy, beliefs about knowledge construction and its connection to human creative agency, and frameworks for meaning making. Each of these comes into prioritized focus even as they are all always influencing practice.

### *Bringing social change into focus*

Groups coming together to change an aspect of their society is, of course, as old as humankind. However, our modern era has given rise to specific theories and practical "schools" of social change that target inequity as it is structured into modern systems, institutions, political practices, and dominant narratives. These schools of change have, at their core, understandings about how change happens. In philanthropy, even charitable giving that seems targeted toward a specific unmet need of individuals (like housing, health care, nutrition) is often grounded in understandings of social change and mechanisms for action.

Change agents in philanthropy may draw from the basic provision focus of the 19th century progressive era efforts that sought to protect workers and children or we may look to the civil rights actions of the 1960s and peaceful resistance and protest. We can embrace pedagogical insights embodied in the work of Freire or turn to the feminist pedagogy of bell hooks or embrace the engagement and organizing principles of the Highlander Center. We can tap into technologically fueled narrative shift practices harnessed through millennial social movement dynamics. Change agents often also ground themselves in a history of spiritual or liberation theory that transcends any specific time period.

Social change theory and practice is vast and my examples are clearly an oversimplification. A great resource for more on social change concepts is the *Encyclopedia of Activism and Social Justice* (Anderson & Herr, 2007) and the multiple scholars and practitioners, from within philanthropy, who are surfacing the ways that philanthropic investment has and can support social change, movements, and democracy (Bartczak, 2014; Reich, 2019; Rourke, 2014; Shaw, 2002).

*Bringing philanthropic strategy into focus*

Beliefs about social change and change practices often reveal themselves in philanthropic "strategy" (Buteau et al., 2009). "New" strategy has become the glitzy currency of philanthropy but often with mixed results (Kania et al., 2014). Although strategic planning as a professional tool might be portrayed as a limited technical skill, strategic thinking, theories of change and adaptive, strategic, and emergent learning are becoming hallmarks of discussions within philanthropy about its own effectiveness and levers (Brest, 2010; Brown, 2012; Darling et al., 2016; Lynn et al., 2014; Patrizi & Heid Thompson, 2011; Stanton & Powell, 2015).

We can explore the facets of philanthropic strategy through various venues like:

- Reports made public by foundations themselves, gathered through archival structures, like the Rockefeller Archive Center
- The first peer-reviewed journal about foundations, *The Foundation Review,* that began publication in 2009.
- Academic and Think Tank research about philanthropy enacted through centers and departments—e.g., Sillerman Center for the Advancement of Philanthropy, Dorothy A. Johnson Center for Philanthropy, Urban Institute.
- Philanthropy membership organizations like PEAK Grantmaking, Grantmakers for Effective Organizations, The Council on Foundations; philanthropy serving organizations like CANDID, Center for Effective Philanthropy, National Committee for Responsive Philanthropy; and numerous affinity groups that prompt conversation and learning in the field like Emerging Practitioners in Philanthropy, Women's Funding Group, Neighborhood Funders Group.

Although philanthropy once was strongly aligned with formalized research demonstrations as in place-based change efforts (O'Connor, 2001; Schmitt, 2015), more recently, reporting within philanthropy has tended to take on an evaluative nature. Evaluations of philanthropy's impact often draw from corporate models of cost benefit analysis, return on investment, and input outcomes logics (Coffman & Beer, 2016) and many times use traditional methods that don't necessarily align with the social change discussed, for example:

- systems change (Foster-Fishman & Long, 2009; Jackson, 2019; Jessup et al., 2016);
- leadership development, community capacity building, and engagement (Giloth, 2018; Heifetz et al., 2004);
- comprehensive community change and collective impact (Kania & Kramer, 2011; Landers et al., 2018);

- network dynamics (Easterling, 2012; Plastrik & Taylor, 2004; Scearce, 2011);
- cross sector collaboration (Lane, 2013);
- social and civic innovation and movements (Masters & Osborn, 2010; Preskill & Beer, 2012; Sirianni & Friedland, 1997).

As equity approaches to philanthropy have begun to focus on structures and intentions (Allen-Meares et al., 2011; Brown et al., 2003; Martinez-Cosio & Bussell, 2013; *Trust Based Philanthropy*; Villanueva, 2018) promising practices in the evaluation arena have sought to expand the parameters. Theory of Change Evaluation (Connell et al., 1995), Empowerment Evaluation (Fetterman et al., 1996), Equitable Evaluation (Dean-Coffey et al., 2014), and various forms of participatory evaluation (Rechtman, 2009) each, in their own time period, have pulled philanthropy toward more action-oriented methodologies.

By re-framing philanthropic research efforts as "knowledge work," I seek to push the boundaries further by recognizing lived experience and shared meaning making as the activating force of knowledge efforts and thus to name knowledge construction as the embodiment of equity.

There are at least four primary indications that the time is right for deepening and expanding philanthropy's knowledge work:

- The increasing frustration with the drain that the focus on more and more evaluative data seems to be having on change efforts—particularly when the data process results in dominant legitimization rather than equitable change (Snibbe, 2006).
- The desire for diversification of methodologies being explored within philanthropic initiatives (Bare, 2010).
- The increasing calls for research about philanthropy itself (Barman, 2017; Curti, 1957; Rogers, 2015) and on its intersection with knowledge endeavors (Frusciante, 2014).
- Another indication of the timing for a deeper understanding of knowledge work is the proliferation of increasingly specialized titles within the grantmaking world.

A quick review of positions in the field surfaced professional titles that included terms related to knowledge work:

- scientific affairs
- research, education and research, community research, research services, research and development
- analytics, relations analytics, capacity building analytics
- advocacy evaluation, measurement and evaluation, evaluation and learning, success measurement, program effectiveness
- strategic learning, learning and engagement, grants and learning, evidence and learning, assessment and learning, learning and reporting
- data management, data systems, data visualization, data discovery, database operation, data standards
- information systems, information technology, content management
- innovation, social impact
- knowledge management, knowledge insights

The above indications, including the variety in titles, are encouraging in that they show an increasing awareness that knowledge construction can be understood in ways that recognize human creative agency and opportunities for social creation.

*Bringing knowledge construction as human creative agency into focus*

Professional socialization is processed through disciplines reified through universities and is often based on traditionally institutionalized categories of scientific inquiry. These disciplines provide theories, central questions, preferred methods, and core curriculum in liberal arts education and infuse these into fields of practice such as public administration, urban planning, social work, and more. A simple taxonomy might include:

Natural Sciences— (e.g., biology, chemistry, and physics)

Arts and Humanities— (e.g., philosophy, history, architecture, design, and literary studies)

Social Sciences —

Anthropology—questions of patterned behavior known as culture

Psychology—observation of individual or community sense of being

Geography—observations of physical place

Sociology—exploration of group interactions

Political Science—examination of power

Economics—questions of distribution of resources

Pedagogy/Learning Sciences—inquiry into development phases

Philanthropic strategy often draws theoretical perspectives and questions from the social sciences. As valuable as these are to understanding *social construction,* for the purpose of social change, it is helpful to capture *knowledge construction* as a process of shared meaning making. Doing so links knowledge construction to social creation (Cox, 2014; Lehrner & Allen, 2008) and solidifies the notion that having the power over one's own creative agency is integral to the realization of equity.

In focusing on knowledge construction and meaning making against the backdrop of both academic discourse and past philanthropic practice, it is important to make a key philosophical distinction. *Learning and knowledge are actually different phenomena.* Often, learning and knowledge are used interchangeably. However, to deeply explore knowledge work, I have found it important to differentiate—conceptually—all the things we may consider "learning" and focus more on the essence of "knowledge." Of course, in practice, our definitions often blur, intersect, or overlap. For purposes here, let's ground ourselves in the following:

**Learning** is a process that we do naturally as human beings that enables us to adapt, adjust, evolve, and survive amidst complexity. We can learn implicitly or reflect on learning explicitly. Learning is about

> pondering and coming to a deeper understanding. It can be formal or informal, designed or serendipitous, individual or collective.
>
> **Knowledge**, however, is socially constructed and located specifically in place and time. It is about actively making meaning in interaction with a social context. Whether knowledge is spoken or not, it is public—it is voiced or expressed outwardly in some way (Frusciante, 2022).

This distinction leads us to an understanding of knowledge as a deeper embodiment of learning that ties together adaptation, shared meaning making, and human action. Although we can identify learning from the individual's perspective, knowledge development is not personal alone. Knowledge is about creating in, and through, shared engagement. Even if individuals are coming to deeper understandings seemingly alone, we are doing so always through interaction with the conceptual frameworks that exist in our communities and society. As we emphasize the engaged and social interaction of knowledge work, we open up the awareness we are always co-creating our understandings of self-*and*-the-world and self-*in*-the world at the same time.

Embracing this awareness does something very important to the discussion of philanthropic initiatives. It expands the discussion to encompass a level of social creativity not often part of an evaluative discussion. Philanthropy's contemporary concerns and investments in social change therefore call for increasingly versatile, flexible, and co-creative framings of knowledge construction.

### *Bringing frameworks and meaning making into focus*

To embrace co-creation, particularly when we are discussing social change, it is important to prioritize meaning making (Lehrner & Allen, 2008) and a notion of "dialectic"—the relationship between part and whole. Although research and analytic processes often privilege the pulling apart of concepts and categorizing the world into smaller and smaller parts, understanding lived experience requires attention to wholeness.

As humans, we are always engaged in active meaning making that seeks to bring together individual concepts, observations, and experiences with a broader sense of the world around us. We both identify and categorize parts and we also seek to form connections and a sense of holism. In combination, both are essential to meaning making.

One way that this dialectic understanding is often missed in philanthropy is in the tendency to transfer programmatic models rather than embrace changes in practice and ways of being. Models, in proposing a series of steps, are developed in one place and time, and then thought to be movable, mostly intact, to other places and times. There is an assumption in philanthropy that demonstrating, through research, that change can happen will prompt the public sector to replicate these models and take them to "scale" to make greater change happen. Much like in the natural sciences, replication has had a hold on philanthropic change efforts for many decades.

Attempts at model transference and scaling overlook or simplify the contextual aspect of change, minimize the influence of lived experience in social change, and reduce human agency to a technical application rather than a creative and constructive role in society. Doing this neglects that human action is always in interaction with a broader social context and that this interaction is actually at the center of social construction and, therefore, social change (Hjelmar, 1996). History has helped us to understand that the deepest social change that truly disrupts inequitable structures hardly ever happens through technical solutions but more so through relationships and emergence (Wheatley & Frieze, 2006).

Unlike models, frameworks embody a respect for emergence by being deeply contextual and grounded in place and time. That said, frameworks are also a way to move insights across space and time and to do this in ways that open up the possibility of change. The movement of understanding happens, not as a series of replicable steps, but through processes of engagement. In this way frameworks move in much the same way they are created—through shared meaning making and broader social interactions.

The following three case examples each demonstrate a deeply engaged approach that begins with "knowledge opportunity scanning" and is marked by the development and progression of frameworks within shared inquiry processes.

### *Transition: Knowledge Work in Practice*

In bringing these conceptual areas into focus, one at a time, we have essentially mapped the core components of an emerging field of knowledge work in philanthropy. Let's now explore how framework building became a practice of knowledge work within equity-centered social change initiatives. A little bit about my location (self-in-the-world) for the purpose of reflection and transparency.

I was raised in a working-class urban neighborhood where people helped their neighbors but never used words like philanthropy and where income was never discretionary. For our family, it was a time when democracy was hopeful even though there was acute awareness of deep imperfections in its practice. I was a first-generation college grad and was raised to notice power differences based on race, class, and gender in particular. I was encouraged to be mindful and conscious about how I used that power although we did not yet have terms like white privilege. I learned first-hand how inequity had direct life outcomes. I was 17 when my mother died of cancer after years of being told that her pains were merely "women's pains" and didn't require medical tests. Over the years, that experience has taken hold for me in a deep commitment to equity and specifically knowledge work as it relates to social change efforts.

Professionally, I have spent more than 25 years in knowledge work in the private, public, and nonprofit sectors and in community organizations, k-12 schooling, academia, nonprofit intermediaries, and philanthropy. I was one of the first people to hold the title of "knowledge development officer" in philanthropy. I entered into philanthropy during an exciting time as foundations were experimenting with targeted positions in knowledge. In a research sense, I take a socio-political stance because I seek understanding of how power and social interaction are intertwined and how knowledge construction can increase equity.

Because of my experience in social change work, I suggest that we are always in a process of scanning. In connection with the conceptual buckets explored above, we are scanning for where change can be activated. I thus begin most client-based partnerships with a process I call "knowledge opportunity scanning," which is based in four assertions.

1. The world is complex and moves quickly and we make decisions by continually scanning our environment.

2. In any system or environment, there are "structures, spaces and pathways" where there are opportunities for shared meaning making. We can identify these opportunities by pointing to:
   - Structures that show up in our own beliefs as well as in our context and our society;

   Spaces where relationships, conversation, and decisions are made;

   Pathways through which power moves and activates change.
3. Change processes are benefited when we acknowledge these structures, spaces, and pathways as inherently socially interactive.
4. These structures, spaces, and pathways are the strategic location for engaged knowledge practice and the starting point for the emergence of conscious and situated methodologies.

The following three case examples all derive from engaged research conducted through an independent contractor agreement specifically to engage in knowledge development. Each began with a knowledge opportunity scan that shows up in more detail in the full partner reports. Here I dive more deeply into the methods and framework building that prompted shared meaning making.

For each case example, I share a brief context for the knowledge partnership; the agreed-upon focus of the knowledge partnership; key methods decisions; description of the shared inquiry process; the sequence of frameworks that emerged through and were grounded in the shared inquiry, and a key insight for the emerging field of knowledge work within philanthropically funded change initiatives.

Complete reports for each case example can be found at: https://kd2change.com/resources/featured-topics/embodying-equity- chapter-examples/

***Case Examples***

*Case Example #1: BEING Together in Knowledge Work*

**Context.** The first case example comes from a private philanthropy effort, funded by a single donor through his local city-wide giving. The donor co-designed the initiative with an experienced equity educator. The Co-creating Effective and Inclusive Organizations (CEIO) initiative's stated mission was:

> CEIO's core intention is to support community-serving organizations and organizers to fully embody inclusivity, justice and conscious co-creation, thereby inspiring, encouraging and expanding the wider practice of these values within the communities they serve.

CEIO provided supports to community serving nonprofits to emphasize that diversity and inclusion are essential to organizational and mission effectiveness. CEIO did this through:

- a series of reflective tools and a shared retreat experience grounded in liberation practices;
- a team of capacity builders who provided intensive diversity, equity, and inclusion supports and partnership with local community-serving organizations;
- a community of practice that brought together partner organization staff (from various roles) in shared learning formats that helped to frame and energize the organizational engagement;
- guest equity practitioners that shared frameworks and practices from mind-body-spirit perspectives;
- funding provided to selected organizations who agreed to a multi-year partnership approach to whole systems change.

Conscious co-creation was at the heart of the CEIO initiative. Concepts of community empowerment, voice, change, and the role of organizers and community-serving organizations grounded the initiative and were the starting place for knowledge efforts as well.

**Focus of the Knowledge Partnership.** When I began working with the initiative, its efforts had been underway for approximately a decade. To begin my exposure and understanding, I took part in a signature retreat that familiarized me with some of the key principles and frameworks that grounded the initiative. Through conversations with the director and participation with the core group of capacity builders and initiatives guides, I became familiar with the intentions, workings, and learning stance of those involved. I also mapped out the various programmatic offerings of the initiative. This immersion, for me, was a process of knowledge opportunity scanning. As I explored the initiative, I was tapping into not just the pieces of the work but also the structures that grounded the work, the various spaces where relationship and conversation were happening, and how power was engaged inside the initiative. These all contributed to discussion about what would be the goal of the knowledge work at that point in time.

As expressed to me by the director, her interest was in "making visible" the whole systems approach of the initiative and particularly its central concept of conscious co-creation.

**Key Methods Decisions.** In conversation and through immersion, the director and I agreed that a shared inquiry approach would be the process most aligned with the CEIO efforts. We moved forward with a combination of my becoming a participant observer in various activities of the initiative and also facilitating a group of 12 individuals in a year-long process.

I provided some basic requests for the selection of the inquiry group. These were based mostly in my capacity (English as my only language) and also past experience in change work. This experience suggested that there are changemakers more or less inclined to formal data-based inquiry work. The group of 12 that were invited and agreed to participate were a combination of capacity builders, staff from current or past organizational partners, and organizers that participated in CEIO programming. Each inquiry participant was provided a stipend or hourly compensation, dependent on their existing employment relationships with the initiative.

Together the group brought diversity beyond the various roles. Individuals in the group brought diversity of age, gender identity, ethnicity, educational level, economic bracket, professional fields (e.g., health, education, social work, nonprofit leadership), and length of time in the initiative. All were deeply familiar with the educational approach and ways of being in the initiative.

**Framework Building.** Once a shared inquiry approach was agreed to, we continued the knowledge work with a focus on lived experience as the core of methodology design, reflection, data, analysis and representation. I began my facilitation role, in my first inquiry meeting with the group, by opening up the question of the meanings of truth, knowledge, inquiry, and research themselves. In a space where all responses were to be okay, I asked the inquiry group to brainstorm these questions:

> What are your notions of truth and how do you experience words like research, knowledge, inquiry?
>
> How do we want to engage together as a group?
>
> What might our processes be in the context of the broader world?
>
> How might story show up in our shared work?

The discussion was far reaching. Sometimes these terms invoked a sense of wonder and exploration; sometimes they stirred up the discomfort of being more or less than; one person noted the connection between knowledge and his grandmother's kitchen and the smell of cookies; for many, there was an awareness of how research, in particular, had been used as a form of oppression in the communities in which they worked or grew up.

Although I did not plan this ahead of time, when I categorized the responses to these questions, they easily aligned with the concepts that academics discuss in developing new methodologies—ontology, epistemology, axiology, methodology, and methods.

With this shared understanding, the group developed inquiry intentions from their own experiences and beliefs about, and desires for, our knowledge process. Taken together, these two frameworks (see Fig. 5.1) served to convey both the way we all were agreeing to show up for "knowingness" and also the ways in which we would hold each other to agreed-upon concepts we believed aligned with trustworthiness and credibility in our inquiry.

Next the group engaged in a process of developing change constructs or "clusters of ideas that coalesce around a concept and occur in various configurations over time" (Frusciante, 2004). Change constructs are similar to themes but they are different in that the goal is not to define a term or create a typology. Rather the analysis lends itself to identifying concepts that need to be discussed, reflected upon, and opened up in efforts toward greater equity. This process can be an important way to surface and engage with lived experience.

The group utilized a prompt format, focused on artifacts and events from their experiences in change processes. The format was similar to how a participant researcher might take field notes. I asked them to describe key events in their change work with an eye toward separating out what they had observed with their five senses, what their reaction to the events had been, and what meaning they were making of the event.

Over multiple inquiry group meetings, members of the group shared their documentation pages and discussed these artifacts and events. We then looked for patterns and linkages across the artifacts and events. We did this by physically moving sheets around the room and then taping them on the walls.

I recorded these conversations, worked with them, and then brought highlights, synopses, and categorizations back to the group. A key aspect here is that I never "named" any of the constructs on my own. My analytic contribution at this stage was to test out the groupings of data and note what I was sensing bubbling up. The group members were responsible for confirming or discussing my interpretation and then ultimately, naming the constructs that they thought were most valuable.

The group members themselves noted how valuable this inquiry process was to them and in their work. They noted how, although they perhaps could have named additional constructs or renamed the chosen ones, that the insights surfaced seemed relevant to other contexts and initiatives beyond this particular one. This was a sign to all of us that we had tapped into enduring principles of change process itself. Another indicator of the power of this work is that, even years later, the inquiry report features prominently on the initiative website and is also being used as an orienting document for people new to the initiative team.

**Insight for the Field.** Two aspects of this knowledge partnership offer elements for the emerging knowledge field in philanthropy. One is that grounding methodology inside the change approach of an initiative offers an incredible opportunity for knowledge work to offer reflective analysis while also contributing to the work of the initiative.

Another is that a change construct process that centers lived experience from the formation of inquiry methodology all the way through to representation of findings is one way that engaged research can contribute to the success of philanthropically funded change initiatives.

Grounded methodology may not be replicable as a model across place and time, but, to the extent that the methodology illuminates change work, it can actually offer deep insights and open up constructs that can be generative and transferable across initiatives and perhaps even relevant in additional institutional and community settings.

### *Case Example #2: Embracing Wholeness in Knowledge Work*

**Context.** The second case example comes from an engagement with a community foundation, specifically a fund for women and girls within the foundation. Fairfield County's Community Foundation Fund for Women & Girls leadership sought to conduct its first "landscape scan" of programs and services for women and girls in the region. Although the foundation had repeatedly contracted for research on demographics and public challenges, their intention was to use the landscape scan to better understand the gaps between needs and available services as a way to make future grantmaking decisions.

**Focus of Knowledge Partnership.** A foundation design team made up of the director of the Fund for Women & Girls, a board member who chaired the foundation's research subcommittee, a foundation vice president focused on strategy, a foundation staff member responsible for data analytics, and an external consultant familiar with the foundation's work. Once the scope of the work was identified, I too added project staff to the team, bringing on a project administration support and a focus group co-facilitator.

**Key Methods Decisions.** The data collection methods designated for the landscape analysis included a basic list of programs and services in the geographic region; a survey sent to grantees of the fund; and focus groups. Three key decisions were made that affected the shape and depth of the landscape scan.

During the discussion of the focus groups, the co-design team agreed to an invitation process that went beyond existing grantees. This meant community partners or volunteers working with nonprofit service providers could provide input as well. Also at each focus group, we specifically asked for names of additional community leaders and organizations to include in the surveys and focus groups. (A full description of the survey list process is in the addendum of the report.) Sometimes called a snowball process, this outreach ensured that

**Figure 5.1:**
*Framing Knowledge Work*

### WHAT WE BELIEVE ABOUT REALITY

**(ONTOLOGY - nature of being, becoming, existence or reality; the branch of metaphysics dealing with the nature of being)**

- Will always learn more and expand the truth
- Truth has many sides
- Nature in a matrix
- What is my nature? - trees and flowers–what is my core - trees and flowers, grass = external and that is hard for all to relate
- Future is made entirely of material from the past
- Nature is more intelligent than us (look for defects - no - drives you crazy) - observe patterns in the world - listen to what that is telling us
- How complicated things get when we put matters in our own hands
- Relationship of self - is connected to the rest of the world
- Efficiency and truth - together they don't go well together - truth in a box works - need to be right not always about truth - image and perception not truth

### HOW DO WE GET TO KNOWING

**(EPISTEMOLOGY - the theory of knowledge, especially with regard to its methods, validity, and scope)**

- Intuition, insight, knowingness, the source, core, center
- Accessible language
- Openness, mindfulness, suspended judgment
- What do I feel like when centered / How do I know/ Makes a practice
- Use of self in patterns and mirror – info within us is useful to the work outside
- Fossils = information that causes ripples
- See alternative processes to conventional thinking – fear of something new – testing new processes and ideas
- Being, energy, mindfulness, awareness to the process
- Intuition vs conventional thinking as we interrogate "what is" ..... body is telling you something is wrong
- If one looks outside of self can shake my core – center – how does one know they are centered

### WHAT DO WE VALUE

**(AXIOLOGY - the study of the nature of value and valuation, and of the kinds of things that are valuable)**

- Can we do visioning without an analysis
- Trusting in process (transparency)
- Response what of accessibility
- The natural world was taken from you and you fuckin deserve to have it back
- How to be purposeful and grounded in goals and process/activities
- Mindfulness/ knowingness "this doesn't feel right" - doesn't have integrity
- Name our positions in our inquiring
- External seeker of truth – our responsibility to find our core and our truth
- Us – where we came into the world – pure – with growth – response – natural to follow energy and harmony of world – evolution being impeded by structure – linear truths – what are the things that get us off path

### OUR PROCESS FOR UNDERSTANDING

**(METHODOLOGY - a body of methods, rules, and postulates employed by a discipline: a particular procedure or set of procedures)**

- Process warm not critical
- How we use language (connect to lived reality, power, awareness)
- Engaged in work of shifting power – root level work
- Look for deeper patterns to see where the deeper ripples are – ripple/trigger may be seen as negative – instead look at it as information in the quest for truth
- Not strive for unity. Inclusive. Differing perspectives within group and outside
- Nature, symmetry/order, reflective, center, math- facts, perceptions, direct experience – look for deeper patterns.
- Not designed, something new – interpret "what is" – a map is not a road
- Establish collective understanding in this space – challenge we all have our own disruptions
- Nature as first teacher – only teacher – on land, disconnect – generational – we are nature – are we our own teachers
- Being open to an expanding sense of truth

### OUR TOOLS AND ACTIONS

**(Methods : a systematic procedure, technique, or mode of inquiry employed by or proper to a particular discipline or art)**

- Visual maps
- Examples of patterns
- Identify/name dominant narratives and look for alternatives
- Everything is a process – a conclusion is not final...
- Small to large, spiral, patterns, symbolism, deeper truth, depth
- When do we reflect/mirror something else

the Fund would tap into a broader spectrum of insights about programming and services.

Another decision was to have meetings with the co-design team at various points within the project. In and of itself, this could have been simply a process check-in. However, because of the engagement orientation of the project leads, these meetings turned into analytic meetings as well with insights generated from an additional diversity of perspectives.

Staffing decisions for the project offered an opportunity to broaden the analysis as well. I brought on a co-facilitator whose lived experience was different than my own in the realms of race, community location, and education level. As importantly, she was also a community leader and director of a grassroots nonprofit. I also hired an administrative support person who happened to be of a younger generational category than those of us on the co-design and facilitation team. Even though her position was predominantly administrative, I dedicated funds for her to access some training in diversity and equity understandings, and she attended the focus groups and was encouraged to participate in the conversations.

This combination of co-facilitators from various backgrounds and roles also emphasized an openness for focus group participants to bring in a wholeness of their lived experience. We specifically asked for participants to share from the perspective of their lived experience as well as their professional positions, but it was important to demonstrate this openness. Each of the research decisions centered a respect for lived experience and wholeness, and invited participants, and co-design team alike (most self-identifying as women) to share from the fullness of their experience.

**Framework Building.** Results of the process were documented in a report, a service inventory, and a separately developed resource list of programs and services in the region. The first level framing was that of the inventory. We began with the typology used by the Fund in their grantmaking and then refined this list based on the survey responses and the focus group input.

The project could have stopped there and made a descriptive contribution to the Fund's efforts. However, the analytic contribution of the knowledge work became the development of a lifecycle framework. During the analysis, it became clear that the discussions about programs and services also were embedded with understandings about the developmental phases of a woman's life and the pressures, expectations, and demands that intersect with racial and socioeconomic realities. These also interact with the biological and social phases of a woman's life (see Fig. 5.2). Although we invited gender diversity in the focus groups, the framework admittedly portrays a cis-gendered interpretation of the participant input.

This understanding and analytic framework building would not have emerged had we not invited input and analysis from the perspective of wholeness and lived experience. The lifecycle lens is one that can be adapted across contexts as it poses a framing rather than specific steps or models for programmatic interventions.

**Insight for the Field.** Even knowledge projects that seem directed toward basic data collection can be designed in ways that encourage a deeper level of analysis and the inclusion of a breadth of diversity and depth of lived experience. These possibilities are surfaced through project oversight decisions as well as staffing, data collection, and analysis process decisions. All of these provided a generative process where an unexpected but key framework was developed that could be used in the current location to inform grantmaking and social change programming beyond the current context.

Another serendipitous contribution, brought to our attention by the focus group participants, was the opportunity to tap into the energy generated through this type of lived experience conversation for network building, mobilization, and future collective action. A key aspect of knowledge work in philanthropically funded change initiatives is to identify the times where knowledge construction, in its relationship building potential, can feed into key network activities that activate change processes.

*Case Example #3 Claiming Agency in Knowledge Work*

**Context.** This third case example involved a multi-year partnership with a nonprofit intermediary in the arts and culture arena. The Cultural Alliance of Fairfield County occupies a key regional network space as both a 501c3 nonprofit, a state line-item funded effort, and as a designated regional service organization of a state arts and culture grantmaking agency. This complexity of location was an important factor in the knowledge process so any framework building needed to incorporate the organization's multiple responsibilities and activity locations.

**Figure 5.2:**
*Framing a Lifecycle for Programming*

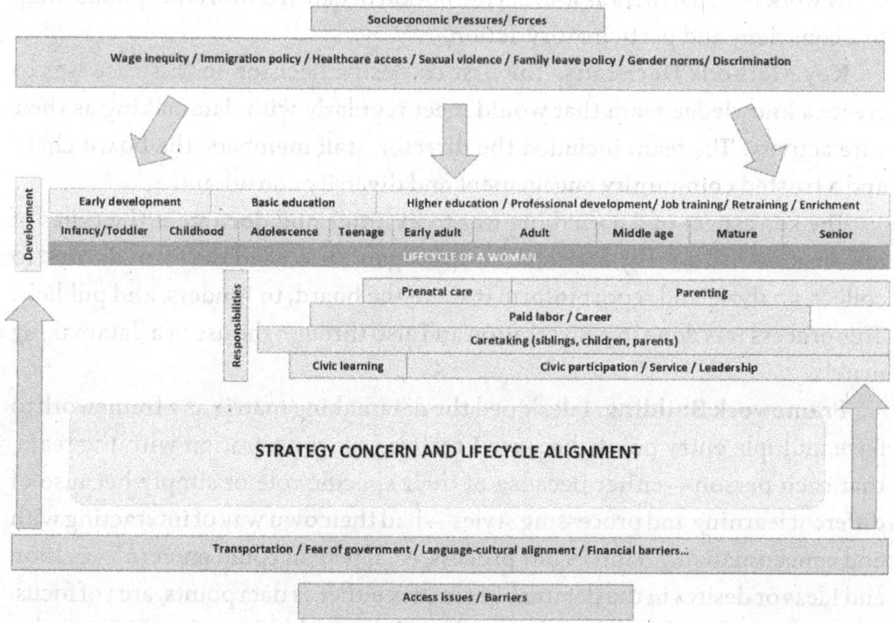


The impetus for knowledge work arose from the organization's desire to prioritize equity as a key lens on the mission and approach of the organization. Although equity had been a design component from the founding of the organization, the region's extreme and increasing wealth disparity and life outcomes gap, along with key social occurrences of the time period, made it even more critical to explicitly amplify the importance of arts and culture in addressing inequity.

**Focus of the Knowledge Partnership.** Initially I volunteered to support the organization's exploration of how an equity lens might contribute to their work. Then, through a retainer agreement, I participated with the staff to begin to examine and increase their equity and inclusion communications and activities. This example, however, emerged from their decision to engage in a targeted meaning making process that would incorporate equity as the focus of knowledge development.

The co-designed knowledge process rested heavily on the notion of "datamaking" (Frusciante, 2022). I developed and now use this terminology as core to my work with partners as it shifts the notion of data from an amorphous thing to a conscious and participatory action.

**Key Methods Decisions.** The first co-design decision in this case was to create a knowledge team that would meet regularly with datamaking as their core activity. The team included the director, staff members, the board chair, and a trusted community engagement and diversity consultant.

The key aspect of datamaking was to examine and document the types of information historically collected by the organization and the formats used to collect, analyze, and report information to the board, to funders, and publicly. This process was done in conversation and also through the use of a datamaking matrix.

**Framework Building.** I designed the datamaking matrix as a framework to have multiple entry points because I realized, in conversation with the team, that each person—either because of their specific role or simply because of different learning and processing styles—had their own way of interacting with and conceptualizing data. In our process, each person could enter information and ideas or desires in the datamaking matrix either as data points, area of focus, or as a desired evidence-based statement they would like to be able to make. They could also add questions about equity and inclusion.

The datamaking matrix had some initial organizing value. The team used the information in the matrix to determine the most important buckets to house indicators that the organization was successful in its work. We termed these "essential categories." These categories themselves were a framework of sorts bounding our discussion. However, even the essential categories were intended to be iterative and changeable within the time constraints of our shared process. We kept all process reports labeled as drafts to acknowledge our openness to re-visit and re-construct throughout our process.

Throughout the process, I continued to use the datamaking matrix to track the notes from our conversation and turn those notes into a technical data plan. However, it quickly became clear that the most generative team conversations were not going to happen in a matrix format.

To shift from a technical focus on data points to a more engaging process of meaning making, I created a discussion format that did three things. It documented agreement on the many different people that the organization had relationships with, by way of its unique position and context. The discussion framework also emphasized that decisions around meaningful indicators, especially with the desire to address structural issue of inequity, did not just come from vision and mission but rather from four core elements of the shared work—core mission, core values, core beliefs, and core functions.

With this framing, we moved forward with discussion, by placing each essential category in this format and together, surfacing indicators that could be collected and would help the organization to notice, document, and share their work (see Fig. 5.3).

The discussion of indicators for each essential category became the basis for:

> a data point list to be used in the design of a data management platform;
>
> real-time alterations to data collection forms like membership registration, feedback, and surveys;
>
> a streamlined analysis plan that focused on places where the same data points could be used as indicators across multiple essential categories.

This example shows that using frameworks to represent shared meaning making can help to encourage group members to reclaim their agency in organizational change processes.

**Insight for the Field.** Although a great emphasis in the social sector is placed on external strategy, embedding equity holistically inside an organization requires an internal focus. Parameters that are often codified in bylaws, on websites, and in board reports as the core of an organization may be even harder to examine and shift than external programs or activities.

From an equitable change perspective, it is important to identify an organization's core mission, beliefs, values, and functions, whether they are documented or simply part of patterned behavior. This process is equally as important to surfacing both a theory of change and also an organization's ways of being.

Knowledge equity work, utilizing framework building as a key element, can support an organization in identifying and aligning its core structures with its commitment to equity and social change. To do so, we need to also recognize that frameworks are fluid and need to be developed, redeveloped, or even set aside based on how effective they are in generating shared meaning making for those involved in the knowledge work.

Doing so requires both a flexibility and also a humility in those of us who have traditionally done the work of framework building in institutional isolation. Knowledge work as engaged research is much messier but also much more generative and immediately significant.

### *Implications and Applications*

Although "knowledge work" doesn't sound as glitzy as "change strategy," it is an embodied and embedded aspect of social change. Knowledge work, as an emerging field within philanthropy, is at a crucial moment in its development. This is an important opportunity to ground the field in both equity principles and practices as integral to knowledge construction itself. The principles of engaged research can ground this field building.

**Figure 5.3:**
*Framing Indicators and Decision-Making*

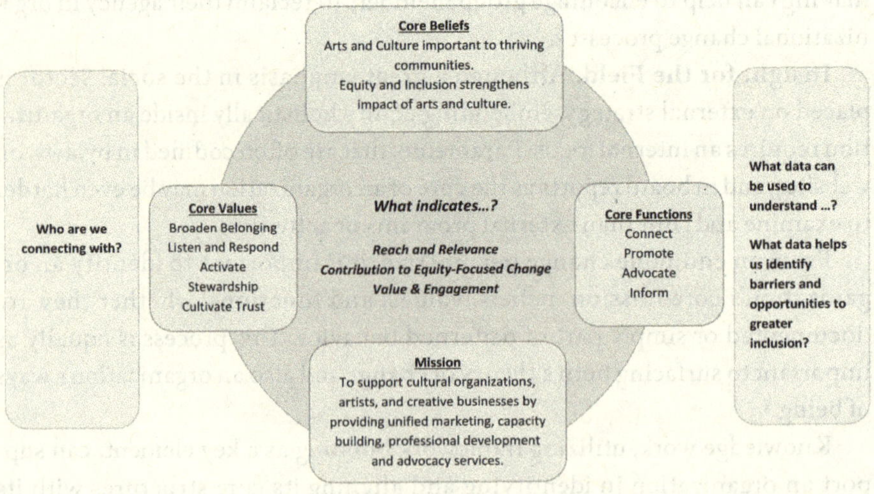

Being effective in knowledge field building calls for us to align methods with the values and rhythms of change strategy, which requires a flexibility that is best accomplished with a deep examination of methods decisions. Seeking to consciously work with methods as intimately aligned with intentions of equitable engagement in knowledge construction is thus important for both transparency and effectiveness.

Knowledge work is always interacting with the structures, spaces, and pathways of the change work within which it is embedded. That is why knowledge opportunity scanning for structures, spaces, and pathways is a key starting point for the co-design of knowledge efforts. From this awareness and deep alignment with change processes, our methodological decisions can make important contributions to change itself.

These three case examples illustrate a way of examining methods decisions that are always intertwined with decisions about who is involved in shared meaning making. In a societal context, philanthropic initiatives provide a valuable space for people to show up as whole and complex and with creative agency to co-create better futures. Never has there been a more generative time in philanthropy—a time energized by the depth of social challenges and the need for co-creation. Knowledge field building and change practice are two sides of the same coin in the invaluable hopefulness of philanthropic partnerships for social change.

## References

Allen-Meares, P., Gant, L., & Shanks, T. (2011). Embedded foundations: Advancing community change and empowerment. *The Foundation Review, 2*(3), 7.

Anderson, G. L., & Herr, K. G. (2007). *Encyclopedia of activism and social justice*. Sage Publications.

Andrews, F. E. (1961). Growth and present status of American foundations. *Proceedings of the American Philosophical Society, 105*(2), 157–161.

Anheier, H. K., & Leat, D. (2013). Philanthropic foundations: What rationales? *Social Research: An International Quarterly, 80*(2), 449–472.

Arno, R., Casteel, L., Guajardo, M., & Mansanares, A. (2012). How inclusion and equity are transforming a foundation and a community. *The Foundation Review, 4*(4), 2.

Auspos, P., Brown, P., Kubisch, A. C., & Sutton, S. (2009). Philanthropy's civic role in community change. *The Foundation Review, 1*(1), 11.

Bare, J. (2010). Philanthropy, evaluation, accountability, and social change. *The Foundation Review, 1*(4), 9.

Barkan, J. (2013). Plutocrats at work: How big philanthropy undermines democracy. *Social Research, 80*(2), 635–652.

Barman, E. (2017). The social bases of philanthropy. *Annual Review of Sociology, 43,* 271–290.

Bartczak, L. (2014). Leveraging a movement moment. *Stanford Social Innovation Review. 12*(2), A22–A23. https://doi.org/10.48558/S7D1-EY04

Bartley, T. (2007). How foundations shape social movements: The construction of an organizational field and the rise of forest certification. *Social Problems, 54*(3), 229–255.

Bell, T. R. (2016). Visually engaged ethnography: Constructing knowledge and critical consciousness. *Journal of Media Practice, 17*(2–3), 126–137.

Berry, J. M. (2005). Nonprofits and civic engagement. *Public Administration Review, 65*(5), 568–578.

Bishop, M. (2013). Philanthrocapitalism: Solving public problems through private means. *Social Research: An International Quarterly, 80*(2), 473–490.

Boyte, H. C. (2011). Constructive politics as public work: Organizing the literature. *Political Theory, 39*(5), 630–660.

Brest, P. (2005). In defense of strategic philanthropy. *Proceedings of the American Philosophical Society, 149*(2), 132–140.

Brest, P. (2010). The power of theories of change. *Stanford Social Innovation Review, 8*(2), 47–51.

Brest, P. (2012). A decade of outcome-oriented philanthropy. *Stanford Social Innovation Review, 10*(2), 42–47.

Brody, E., & Tyler, J. (2012). *How public Is private philanthropy? Separating reality from myth* (2nd ed.). Philanthropy Roundtable.

Brown, P. (2012). Changemaking: Building strategic competence. *The Foundation Review, 4*(1), 8.

Brown, P., Chaskin, R. J., Hamilton, R., Richman, H., Patrizi, P., Sherwood, K., & Spector, A. (2003). Toward greater effectiveness in community change. In J. DeFilippis and S. Saegert (Eds.), *The community development reader* (pp. 150–158). Routledge.

Buteau, E., Buchanan, P., & Brock, A. (2009). *Essentials of foundation strategy.* Center for Effective Philanthropy.

Choudry, A. (2009a). Learning in social action: Knowledge production in social movements. *McGill Journal of Education/Revue des sciences de l'éducation de McGill, 44*(1).

Choudry, A. (2009b). Learning in social action: Knowledge production in social movements/ Apprendre via l'action sociale: La production de Connaissances au sein des mouvements sociaux. *McGill Journal of Education/Revue des sciences de l'éducation de McGill, 44*(1).

Coffman, J., & Beer, T. (2016). How do you measure up? Finding fit between foundations and their evaluation functions. *The Foundation Review, 8*(4), 6.

Coffman, J., Beer, T., Patrizi, P., & Heid Thompson, E. (2013). Benchmarking evaluation in foundations: Do we know what we are doing? *The Foundation Review, 5*(2), 5.

Connell, J. P., Fulbright-Anderson, K., Kubisch, A. C., & Aspen Institute. Roundtable on Comprehensive Community Initiatives for Children and, Families. (1995). *New approaches to evaluating community initiatives.* Aspen Institute.

Cox, L. (2014). Movements making knowledge: a new wave of inspiration for sociology? *Sociology, 48*(5), 954–971.

Cunningham, G. L., Avner, M. L., & Justilien, R. (2014). The urgency of now: Foundations' role in ending racial inequity. *The Foundation Review, 6*(1), 6.

Curti, M. (1957). The history of American philanthropy as a field of research. *The American Historical Review, 62*(2), 352–363.

Darling, M., Guber, H., Smith, J., & Stiles, J. (2016). Emergent learning: A framework for whole-system strategy, learning, and adaptation. *The Foundation Review, 8*(1), 8.

Dean-Coffey, J., Casey, J., & Caldwell, L. D. (2014). Raising the bar–integrating cultural competence and equity: equitable evaluation. *The Foundation Review, 6*(2), 8.

Ealy, L. T., & Ealy, S. D. (2006). Progressivism and philanthropy. *The Good Society, 15*(1), 35–42.

Easterling, D. (2012). Building the capacity of networks to achieve systems change. *The Foundation Review, 4*(2), 5.

Eikenberry, A. M. (2006). Philanthropy and governance. *Administrative Theory & Praxis, 28*(4), 586–592.

Eikenberry, A. M., & Kluver, J. D. (2004). The marketization of the nonprofit sector: Civil society at risk? *Public Administration Review, 64*(2), 132–140.

Ferris, J. (2017). Philanthropy as a catalyst. In: *Stanford Social Innovation Review.* 15(1), A10–A13. https://doi.org/10.48558/VB35-C105

Fetterman, D. M., Kaftarian, S., & Wandersman, A. (1996). *Empowerment evaluation: Knowledge and tools for self-assessment and accountability.* Sage.

Fisher, D. (1983). The role of philanthropic foundations in the reproduction and production of hegemony: Rockefeller foundations and the social sciences. *Sociology, 17*(2), 206–233.

Foster-Fishman, P., & Long, R. (2009). The challenges of place, capacity, and systems change: The story of yes we can! *The Foundation Review, 1*(1), 6.

Francis, M. M. (2019). The price of civil rights: Black lives, white funding, and movement capture. *Law & Society Review, 53*(1), 275–309.

Frusciante, A. (2014). Shifting from "evaluation" to valuing: A six-year example of philanthropic practice change and knowledge development. *The Foundation Review, 6*(2), 21.

Frusciante, A. (2022). *Embodying equity inside and out: A knowledge strategy course for changemakers.* https://knowledgedesign.thinkific.com/courses/embodying-equity-inside-and-out

Frusciante, A. K. (2004). *An analytic case study of the evaluation reports of a comprehensive community initiative.* College Park, MD: University of Maryland.

Giloth, R. (2018). Philanthropy and community engagement. *National Civic Review, 107*(2), 26–36.

Giving-USA. (2022). *Total U.S. charitable giving remained strong in 2021, reaching $484.85 billion.* IUPUI. https://philanthropy.iupui.edu/news-events/news-item/giving-usa:--total-u.s.-charitable-giving-remained-strong-in-2021,-reaching-$484.85-billion html?id=392#:~:text=Giving%20USA%3A%20Total%20U.S.%20charitable,in%20 2021%2C%20reaching%20%24484.85%20billion&text=Giving%20USA%202022%3A %20The%20Annual,to%20U.S.%20charities%20in%202021

Gugerty, M. K., & Karlan, D. (2018). Ten reasons not to measure impact–and what to do instead. *Stanford Social Innovation Review, 8*, 41–47.

Hagerty, R. (2012). *The role of foundations in the changing world of philanthropy: A Houston perspective.* Antioch University.

Hall, P. D. (2006). A historical overview of philanthropy, voluntary associations, and nonprofit organizations in the United States, 1600–2000. *The Nonprofit Sector: A Research Handbook, 2*, 32–65.

Heifetz, R. A., Kania, J. V., & Kramer, M. R. (2004). Leading boldly. *Stanford Social Innovation Review, 2*(3), 20–32.

Hjelmar, U. (1996). Constructivist analysis and movement organizations: Conceptual clarifications. *Acta Sociologica, 39*(2), 169–186.

Jackson, A. D. (2019). *Leveraging Philanthropy in a Systems-Change Initiative.* Doctoral dissertation, Harvard University.

Jessup, P., Parsons, B., & Moore, M. (2016). Partnerships, paradigms, and social-system change. *The Foundation Review, 8*(2), 6.

Kania, J., & Kramer, M. (2011). *Collective impact. Stanford Social Innovation Review, 9*(1), 36–41. https://doi.org/10.48558/5900-KN19

Kania, J., Kramer, M., & Russell, P. (2014). Strategic philanthropy for a complex world. *Stanford Social Innovation Review, 12*(3), 26–33.

Karl, B. D., & Katz, S. N. (1981). The American private philanthropic foundation and the public sphere 1890–1930. *Minerva*, 236–270.

Karlström, M., Brown, P., Chaskin, R., & Richman, H. (2009). Embedded philanthropy and the pursuit of civic engagement. *The Foundation Review, 1*(2), 6.

Kinarsky, A. R., & Christie, C. A. (2022). Analysis of evaluation policies in the philanthropic sector. *American Journal of Evaluation, 43*(2), 175–192.

Kluver, J. D. (2004). Disguising social change: The role of nonprofit organizations as protective masks for citizen participation. *Administrative Theory & Praxis, 26*(3), 309–324.

Landers, G., Price, K., & Minyard, K. (2018). Developmental evaluation of a collective impact initiative: insights for foundations. *The Foundation Review, 10*(2), 10.

Lane, A. (2013). *Eradicating poverty through cross-sector community collaboration.*

Lehrner, A., & Allen, N. E. (2008). Social change movements and the struggle over meaning-making: A case study of domestic violence narratives. *American Journal of Community Psychology, 42*, 220–234.

Lenkowsky, L. (2007). Big philanthropy. *The Wilson Quarterly (1976-), 31*(1), 47–51.

Lynn, J., Kahn, R., Chung, P., & Downes, S. (2014). If you build it, they will come: Creating the space and support for real-time strategic learning. *The Foundation Review, 5*(4), 6.

Martinez-Cosio, M., & Bussell, M. R. (2013). *Catalysts for change: 21st century philanthropy and community development*. Routledge.

Masters, B., & Osborn, T. (2010). Social movements and philanthropy: How foundations can support movement building. *The Foundation Review, 2*(2), 3.

O'Connor, A. (2001). *Poverty knowledge: Social science, social policy, and the poor in twentieth-century U.S. history*. Princeton University Press.

Patrizi, P. (2006). *The evaluation conversation: A path to impact for foundation boards and executives*. Foundation Center.

Patrizi, P., & Heid Thompson, E. (2011). Beyond the veneer of strategic philanthropy. *The Foundation Review, 2*(3), 6.

Pevnick, R. (2013). Democratizing the nonprofit sector. *Journal of Political Philosophy, 21*(3), 260–282.

Plastrik, P., & Taylor, M. (2004). Network power for philanthropy and nonprofits. http://www.barrfoundation.org/files/Netork_Power_for_Philanthropy_and_Nonprofits.pdf

Preskill, H., & Beer, T. (2012). *Evaluating social innovation*. Network Impact and Center for Evaluation Innovation.

Rechtman, J. (2009). A road made by walking: participatory evaluation and social change. *The Foundation Review, 1*(2).

Redwood, Y., & King, C. J. (2014). Integrating racial equity in foundation governance, operations, and program strategy. *The Foundation Review, 6*(1), 5.

Reich, R. (2019). Philanthropy in the service of democracy. *Stanford Social Innovation Review, 17*(1), 26–33.

Reyna, V., Villegas, R., Simrak, M., & Kwakwa, M. (2021). Ethical complexities of civically engaged research. *PS: Political Science & Politics, 54*(4), 734–737.

Rogers, R. (2015). Why the social sciences should take philanthropy seriously. *Society, 52*, 533–540.

Rourke, B. (2014). Philanthropy and the limits of accountability: A relationship of respect and clarity. PACE, Charles F. Kettering Foundation. Belgium. Retrieved from https://policycommons.net/artifacts/1847649/philanthropy-and-the-limits-of-accountability/2593965/CID: 20.500.12592/f2h4nz.

Scearce, D. (2011). Catalyzing networks for social change: A funder's guide. *Grantmakers for Effective Organizations & Monitor Institute*. Retrieved from: https://jimjosephfoundation.org/wp-content/uploads/2012/01/Catalyzing_Networks_for_Social_Change.pdf

Schensul, J. (2010). 2010 Malinowski award engaged universities, community based research organizations and third sector science in a global system. *Human Organization, 69*(4), 307–320.

Schmitt, M. (2015). Philanthropy, politics and democracy. *Society, 52*(6), 549–551.

Shaw, A. (2002). *Social justice philanthropy: An overview.* Prepared for the Synergos Institute, New York.

Sirianni, C., & Friedland, L. (1997). Civic innovation & American democracy. *Change: The Magazine of Higher Learning, 29*(1), 14–23.

Snibbe, A. C. (2006). Drowning in data. *Stanford Social Innovation Review, 4*(3), 39–45.

Stanton, A. B., & Powell, A. (2015). Adventures in adaptation. *Stanford Social Innovation Review, 13*(2), 57–58.

Thomson, D. E. (2022). Foundations of influence: Intervention pathways of foundation influence on city governance and policy. *Nonprofit and Voluntary Sector Quarterly, 52*(5).

*Trust Based Philanthropy.* https://www.trustbasedphilanthropy.org/

Udani, A., & Dobbs, K. L. (2021). The praxis of partnership in civically engaged research. *PS: Political Science & Politics, 54*(4), 725–729.

Van Zandt, S., Newman, G., Lee, C., Jourdan, D., & Ye, X. (2022). Engaged Research: Inviting Residents into the Scientific Process. *Journal of Planning Education and Research, 42*(3), 258–259.

Villanueva, E. (2018). *Decolonizing wealth: Indigenous wisdom to heal divides and restore balance.* Berrett-Koehler Publishers.

Wallerstein, N. (2021). Engage for equity: advancing the fields of community-based participatory research and community-engaged research in community psychology and the social sciences. *American Journal of Community Psychology, 67*(3–4), 251–255.

Wheatley, M., & Frieze, D. (2006). Using emergence to take social innovation to scale. *The Berkana Institute, 9*(3), 147–197.

Young, A., Love, J., Csuti, N., & King, C. J. (2017). Looking in the mirror: Equity in practice for philanthropy. *The Foundation Review, 9*(4), 11.

CHAPTER 6

# How Research Uplifted Youth Visions for Care and Racial Justice in Californians for Justice's Relationship Centered Schools Campaign

*May Lin*

ON A BRIGHT, sunny day in May 2018, over 100 Black, Latinx, Asian American, SWANA (Southwest Asian and North African), Native Hawaiian/Pacific Islander, Native American, and white students and adult allies converged on the steps of California's state capitol in Sacramento. Sporting eye-catching yellow t-shirts emblazoned with "Californians for Justice" and adorned with black and brown silhouettes of protest signs, attendees clasped vibrant yellow and green signs and a large banner with bold capital fonts: "End Racism in Schools Now!" and "Reclaim the Dream of Brown v. Board." Californians for Justice (CFJ) is a "statewide youth-powered organization fighting for racial justice," which believes that "young people are the leaders we need to create the healthy, just, and vibrant schools all of our communities deserve." Joined by allied educational justice organizing and policy advocacy groups, the animating collective drive of the day was to reframe CFJ's Relationship Centered Schools campaign with a reinvigorated focus on relationships as a solution to systemic racism and to compel lawmakers to pass several bills that would help bring to fruition the deferred dreams of Brown vs. Board of Education.

Youth leader Sierra from San Jose kicked off the press conference with the reminder that Linda Brown and civil rights organizers had envisioned an education system that would provide the possibility for all students, regardless of race, to succeed. Yet, as Sierra pointed out: "As a state, we have fallen short of

Linda's dreams. While we have made progress, California schools are still separate and still unequal." Sierra proceeded to cite from an accompanying research brief that CFJ was also publicly sharing for the first time that day (Why Race and Relationships Matter in California Schools): "In California, 1 in 5 Latinx students do not graduate with their class. For Black students, that number is 1 in 3. Pacific Islanders, Filipinos, and Southeast Asians report lower expectations from school staff and stereotyping as failures or gang members." Seamlessly picking up the thread, youth leader Angelo added: "For some people, these are statistics. But for us, these are our lives. Our futures. We're here today because we must talk about race and institutional racism in our education system." Angelo went on to discuss personal experiences of institutional racism in high school as a microcosm of "continued disinvestment in [our] public schools, of Black and Brown students just like me! Today we're saying this is unacceptable. Racism, your time is up!"

Angelo, Sierra, and other CFJ youth leaders and adults did their part that day to stop the clock on racism and usher in a new epoch. They emphatically illustrated that Black and Brown youth are the leaders we desperately need—not just in the future, but also in the immediate present. When youth leaders walked through the doors of state lawmaker offices, they were fully prepared to testify, fortified by the caring support of adult organizers who cultivated their confidence in the multiple types of knowledge they bear. Such knowledge included painfully real lived experiences of systemic injustices, to critical analysis and research informed by political education workshops and the glossy Race and Relationships report they shared with legislators. Their message was loud and clear—racism is not merely an artifact, nor limited to pathologically extreme bigots, and it is not reducible to socioeconomic class. Instead, youth, in their testimonies and in the research report, asserted that dismantling racism requires confronting race head-on, using the solutions devised and implemented by youth. The Relationship Centered Schools campaign, after all, was based on extensive research, outreach, and organizing. Investing in the school staff and structures to cultivate relationships, CFJ youth leaders argued, was essential for tearing down the walls that racism built, and instead building something beautiful and new where all students can flourish.

This day reflected CFJ's Relationship Centered Schools campaign more broadly and the ways that research can support youth organizing. This chapter states in no uncertain terms that research is only one prong of organizing; I align myself with Serrano and colleagues (2022) who argue that "for research to be truly community engaged, it must support the community in transforming relationships of power" (Serrano et al., 2022, p. 5). I draw upon my role as Research Fellow with Californians for Justice from 2014–2020, especially in our collaborative development of the Relationship Centered Schools toolkit, to highlight how research can uplift youth knowledge to win systems change by dismantling carceral logics, adult assumptions, and centering youth visions for care for their humanity. First, CFJ's research centers student voice by uplifting young people's knowledge, challenging how traditional educational research can often confirm preconceived, narrow solutions. Instead, CFJ youth leaders have unapologetically expressed their feelings, analyses, and dreams, regardless of what adults deem appropriate, to carve out imaginative possibilities of transformation. Second, research supported CFJ's narrative change work to ground their campaign in a firmly unwavering critique of structural racism and to be guided by the north star of racial justice, rather than acquiesce to obfuscations or denials of racism. Third, research supported campaign demands towards structural investments in care and processes of developing allies with teachers and administrators. Instead of putting the onus of relationships on already severely overburdened teachers, youth insist that dramatic institutional change is necessary to care for staff and youth alike. Ultimately, this chapter shows that research is not in and of itself an end goal or a source of change in isolation—but it can also play a key role in buoying youth of color-led transformative campaigns.

## Background: Californians for Justice and the Relationship Centered Schools Campaign

CFJ is a statewide youth-led racial and educational justice organization with chapters in Fresno, Long Beach, Oakland, and San Jose. Like other youth organizing groups, it arose in the mid-1990s in response to a slew of attacks on immigrant and communities of color and increased criminalization of youth of color (HoSang, 2010; Pastor, 2018). CFJ's base of youth leaders is cross-racial, with mostly low-income Black, Latinx, and Asian American youth. Like other youth organizing groups, CFJ builds the leadership of those most impacted by educational and racial injustices to create systemic change through campaigns that fight for concrete policy and institutional change. CFJ engages in leadership training and civic education to develop youth leaders' power: including political education and critical civics education where youth understand the root causes of issues they face; developing key leadership skills such as public speaking, voter engagement, and research; and supporting youths' holistic well-being through mentorship, healing, self-care, and academic resources (Terriquez, 2017; Terriquez & Lin, 2016).

When I first got involved as a volunteer in 2014, CFJ was coming off the heels of a 10-year-long coalitional campaign that won a major policy change in equitable funding for K-12 public schools—the Local Control Funding Formula (LCFF).[1] The organization then launched a Student Voice campaign to require that students be engaged in decision-making around the spending of LCFF funds. In 2015, CFJ was ready for a new campaign. To chart their next path, youth across the state conducted action research to answer the question: "What key resources do California students, especially low-income youth of color, need to prepare them for 21st century college & careers?" After surveying 2000 students and conducting a literature review and focus groups, convenings and interviews with parents, educators, and policy experts, youth leaders concluded that "school staff and teachers are the most important resources," and that caring adults are critical to student success. However, they also found that structural disinvestments leave teachers feeling overwhelmed and unequipped to fully care for students, engendering a need for broader systemic change to support relationship building in schools.

Eventually, this research became the foundation for the Relationship Centered Schools campaign, including demands such as: investing in staff, creating space for relationship-building, and valuing student voice. For example, as of Spring 2023, five high schools in Long Beach have committed to becoming Relationship Centered Schools driven by racial equity (Esqueda, 2023). These schools have created "design teams," centering students of color leadership in partnership with administrators, teachers, and parents. Students have led activities such as peer to peer interviews, classroom observations, school-wide cultural fairs, and professional development to center students' voices and recommendations for classroom instruction and pedagogy. While this work is ongoing, thus far student leaders have shaped commitments from their schools such as increasing support, resources, and accountability for Black students, and providing concrete opportunities for BIPOC students to share perspectives with the Instructional Leadership Team.

I became integrated into this campaign, both on a local level in the Long Beach chapter and in the statewide research. I continued my work as a volunteer supporting the local chapter with youth tutoring, political education, leadership development, and other needs such as transportation, while also taking on a more formalized role as a research fellow in 2017 to help CFJ develop a "Relationship Centered Schools toolkit." This chapter draws from and refers to the following toolkit items that I collaborated with in CFJ, as summarized in Table 6.1.

**Table 6.1: Overview of Research Supporting the Relationship Centered Schools (RCS) Campaign**

| Research Product | Overview | Data | Campaign Context |
|---|---|---|---|
| RCS Actions and Services Deck ("Relationship Centered Schools Programs and Practices, n.d.) | Examples of compelling models of RCS solutions and research evidence of efficacy | Best practices from existing models | Supported districts in implementing RCS |
| Oakland Teacher Retention Report ("Relationship Centered Schools: Teacher Retention Starts with Relationships," 2018) | Highlighted systemic issues behind teacher of color recruitment, hiring, and retention, including literature review & solutions aligned with RCS | Oakland student leaders conducted surveys on teacher retention with 84 teachers, interviews with 5 principals and education policymakers, and focus groups with 8 teachers and 60 students | Part of CFJ Oakland's campaign to invest in teachers, including advocating for programs to reduce class sizes, train new teachers, and provide teacher collaboration time |
| Race and Relationships Brief ("Why Race & Relationships Matter in California Schools," 2018) | Aimed towards education policy makers, allies, and other key influencers. Outlined connection between racial equity and relationships as linked to multiple issues and bodies of scholarship | Mostly a literature review, including student stories and letters to racism | Supported re-launch of CFJ's RCS campaign with a greater focus on racial justice and equity, used in delegation meetings during Sacramento statewide action |

| Research Product | Overview | Data | Campaign Context |
| --- | --- | --- | --- |
| Lesbian, Gay, Bisexual, and Queer and Trans/Gender Nonconforming (LGBQ and TGNC) Students report ("Why Relationship Centered Schools Matter For Lesbian, Gay, Bisexual, Queer/Transgender and Gender Non-Conforming Students," 2018) | Report about intersecting challenges and specific RCS solutions for queer, trans, and gender nonconforming youth, especially youth of color | Conducted literature review and a focus group that highlighted students' experiences and priorities for solutions | Part of efforts to uplift RCS solutions in relationship to intersectionality and specific student populations |
| English Language Learner Report (unpublished/not publicly available) | Unpublished report about specific RCS solutions for English Language Learners | Conducted literature review and interviews with four English Learners in CFJ and four staff | Meant to highlight specific voice and agency of English Learners to align with statewide advocacy including the English Learner roadmap |
| Baseline Research for a Longer-Term Evaluation (private internal document) | Research to support CFJ's grantseeking for a 3-year-long evaluation of youth-led Relationship Centered practices, programs, and policies | Preliminary research from July–November 2018. With another research partner, we conducted 31 interviews with administrators, teachers, and students from 11 high school sites in CFJ's four districts across California | Part of effort to study and collect data about the influence of CFJ's youth organizing efforts and deeper understandings of school transformation processes |

A significant component of research involved searching for existing "bright spot" models and documenting best practices and challenges of new initiatives won by CFJ. The Oakland chapter asked me to explore extant examples where students play a role in teacher and staff hiring and orientation to inform their own local demands. As Ishida, statewide strategy consultant explained, this type of research could "support the concept of modeling small scale changes to create big scale shifts." (J Ishida, personal communication, July 25, 2019). For example, when CFJ would win the inclusion of students on a teacher hiring committee, they explained that this could create "an opening to shift perceptions and to expand the terrain of 'safe/appropriate' roles for youth in schools which then leads to the bigger shifts in culture/practices." More broadly, this vision for transformation centers students leading together and sharing decision-making power with adults towards more equitable practices. The design teams described above are an example, as are other dimensions of CFJ's work, such as students in Oakland winning a say in hiring decisions for teachers in the district and a statewide victory of $3 billion in the California State Budget for community schools, which CFJ has argued must become sites for centering young people most impacted by oppression in shared decision-making (Ignacio, 2022).

Meanwhile, literature reviews also helped to support narrative change and campaign framing with validation and legitimacy. CFJ staff brought in their expertise around the current state of the field: for example, for the Race and Relationships brief, Taryn, the Executive Director, pointed out the need to align with current educational policy interests in neuroscience and improvement science. J. pointed out that decision-makers often dismiss national studies, prompting a focus on California-specific studies. Staff also pushed me to make sure that we included disaggregated data for multiple racial groups, and to truly center student voice and agency rather than getting caught up in the ubiquity of oppression. Thus, although the research itself was not always truly participatory or youth-led, research was nevertheless a part and parcel of broader campaign strategy in the following ways I outline.

## How Research Uplifts Student Voice

Research in the Relationship Centered Schools campaign amplified young people's voices and expertise in ways that often challenged the idea that adults are the main bearers of wisdom. After all, CFJ's campaign wins should not be confined to ink on paper—they are also meant to engender dramatic cultural shifts in how youth of color are perceived. Racist, adultist, classist, homophobic assumptions of youth of color work to persistently stall implementation of racial equity wins. Staff and youth told me consistently that administrators believe that "young people don't know what they need." As former organizer Nancy pointed out: "We have to start changing the way that adults think about youth of color too. . . . We have to change the culture so that students are seen as valuable decision-makers" (Fieldnotes, February 17, 2015). The RCS campaign, following a throughline of CFJ's work, sought to reframe students of color as the genuine experts that they are. After all, as young people often pointed out in explaining the campaign: "who knows best how effective or good a teacher is than those who are actually going through it?" (Fieldnotes, October 2, 2018).

Research in the RCS campaign contributed to this cultural shift in the following ways: first, youth-led research exemplifies how Black and Brown youth are knowledge producers and leaders, challenging hierarchical positioning of adult researchers as sole bearers of legitimate knowledge. Second, research uplifts young people's diagnoses of what is fundamentally wrong in schools, including their emotional and felt experiences—refusing respectability politics to show that how they feel in school does indeed matter. Third, research validates young people's expansive visions and priorities that refuse to be stifled by limited adult imaginations.

CFJ's youth-led action research has expanded both diagnoses and prescriptions of solutions to educational ills. In their 2015 action research, youth showed that engaging their peers, teachers, and administrators with genuine curiosity could plant the seeds for a campaign that was unexpected to adults, but fully rooted in young people's lived experiences. Indeed, adults initially responded to CFJ youth leader findings on the importance of caring adults in schools with marked skepticism. As then-Executive Director Taryn noted, she had expected the action research to uncover desires for a campaign that would align closely with previous efforts around school funding, or another similar policy in the vein of previous campaigns around testing or more counselors that seemed more intuitively linked to educational attainment. Students' research that highlighted how caring adults are definitional and central, not auxiliary to teaching, caught her off guard. As Taryn implied, the focus on emotional well-being and relationships as critical to student of color success was a dramatic shift. But, because of CFJ's ethos of following the lead of youth, she recognized the need to listen. As a result, she pointed out that students ignited the normalization of social emotional learning, whole child frameworks, and other approaches in educational policy.

Importantly, this highlights how youth-led research can challenge still-dominant ideas of adult, external researchers "as omniscient narrators empowered by an authorial voice" (Staley, 2018, p. 295) and forms of research that "are used to confirm preexisting beliefs and support existing policies" (Orum Hernández

& Barcelos, 2023, p. 92), thus foreclosing more expansive transformation. Young people's research rankled adult sensibilities, and revealed how their knowledge as insight, when listened to and valued, could provide a much-needed shake up to well-worn practices. Their disruption was not always welcome: students visited school board members to discuss their campaign and were met with what they described as immediate dismissiveness. They recounted a school board member as believing that students were "talking bad about the teachers . . . She [the school board member said], there's no teacher that doesn't care!" (Fieldnotes, July 10, 2019). Student-led research, of course, found not only that this claim was untrue, but also reflected their efforts to shift the frame from individual "bad apples" to systemic contexts that enable and/or disable care, as discussed more in the third section.

Furthermore, research in the campaign context means truly embracing how Black and Brown young people think, speak, and feel without having to contort themselves into white, middle-class norms. As then-CFJ staff Saa'un P. Bell wrote in the Race and Relationships (2018) brief, "unearthing students' internalized racism begins with valuing them—seeing them as whole and unbroken, brimming with potential, experts capable of teaching and learning" (p. 2). In addition to equipping young people with the types of statistics and research that adult decision-makers valued, our research also unapologetically centered young people's deeply felt experiences, such as the spiritual and emotional tolls enacted by structural racism and disinvestment. Consider, for example, this from the Race and Relationships brief. Figure 6.1 shows the interweaving of multiple types of knowledge—first and foremost, Raquel's and Naudika's experiences make evident that how schools dehumanize Black and Brown young people, with toxicity worming its ways into their psyches, is not merely a matter of young people's emotional fragility, as adults may often express. Instead, their observations illustrated how systemic racism spans multiple levels and jumps scale—even if the feeling might be individual, clearly they are also undergirded by intersecting forces of policy and institutional oppression.

Finally, research uplifts youth of color's brilliance and innovation that cannot be contained by victim or deficiency-ridden narratives. See, for example, Figure 6.2, an excerpt from the LGBQ/TGNC brief, which highlights solutions that CFJ leaders prioritized during our focus group discussion. Young people in places like Santee High School have already been not only dreaming up, but

**Figure 6.1:**
*Excerpt from the Race and Relationship Brief*

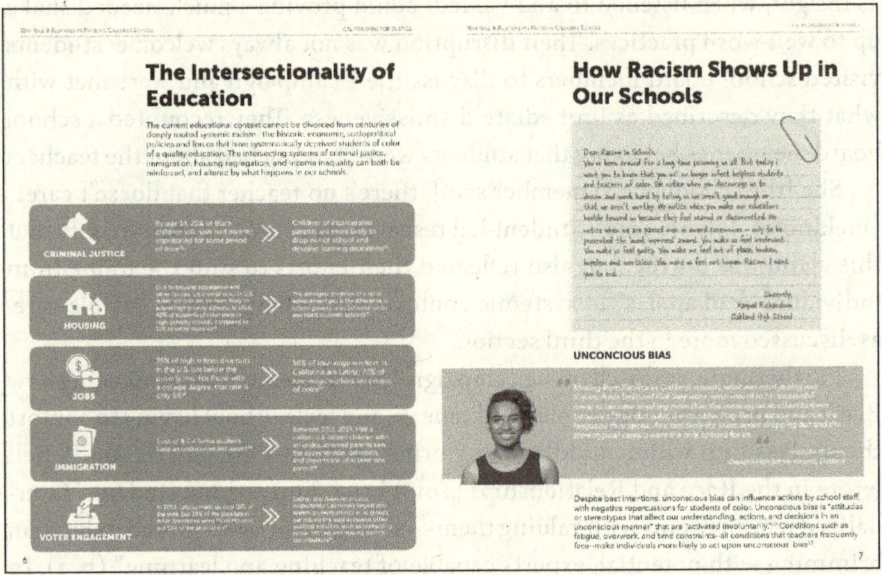

## The Intersectionality of Education

The current educational context cannot be divorced from centuries of deeply rooted systemic racism—the historic, economic, sociopolitical policies and forces that have systematically deprived students of color of a quality education. The intersecting systems of criminal justice, immigration, housing segregation, and income inequality can both be reinforced, and altered by what happens in our schools.

CRIMINAL JUSTICE

HOUSING

JOBS

IMMIGRATION

VOTER ENGAGEMENT

6

## How Racism Shows Up in Our Schools

Dear Racism in Schools,
You've been around for a long time poisoning us all. But today I want you to know that you will no longer infect helpless students and teachers of color. We notice when you discourage us to dream and work hard by telling us we aren't good enough or that we aren't worthy. We notice when you make our educators hostile toward us because they feel scared or discomforted. We notice when we are passed over in award ceremonies – only to be presented the 'most improved' award. You make us feel irrelevant. You make us feel guilty. You make me feel out of place, broken, hopeless and worthless. You make us feel not human. Racism, I want you to end.

Sincerely,
Kanyel Richardson
Oakland High School

UNCONCIOUS BIAS

Despite best intentions, unconscious bias can influence actions by school staff, with negative repercussions for students of color. Unconscious bias is "attitudes or stereotypes that affect our understanding, actions, and decisions in an unconscious manner" that are "activated involuntarily."[16] Conditions such as fatigue, overwork, and time constraints—all conditions that teachers frequently face—make individuals more likely to act upon unconscious bias[17].

7

making very real institutional changes such as gender-neutral restrooms that others might deem unthinkable or impossible. Students also emphasized the importance of inclusive curriculum. From CFJ, they knew that Eurocentric curriculum and accompanying European norms of gender and sexuality are far from inevitable. Instead, historizing and decolonizing gender and sexuality could resist erasures in a thoroughly intersectional way, and further highlight full expansiveness in ways to be, love, and act in relationship to each other.

Another example can be found in our unpublished brief on English Language Learners, based on interviews with CFJ leaders, which centered around the cultural wealth of English Language Learners as the heart of California's celebrated rich diversity who wield multiple skills and knowledge to deftly navigate varied linguistic, cultural spaces. We wanted to highlight how CFJ leaders who are English Learners are already creating spaces that are more inclusive, even if their labor and leadership are not recognized—for example, by translating for their parents, family, and community members and providing lifelines to other immigrant students who are in jeopardy of falling through the cracks.

**Figure 6.2:**
*Excerpt from LGBT/TGNC Brief*

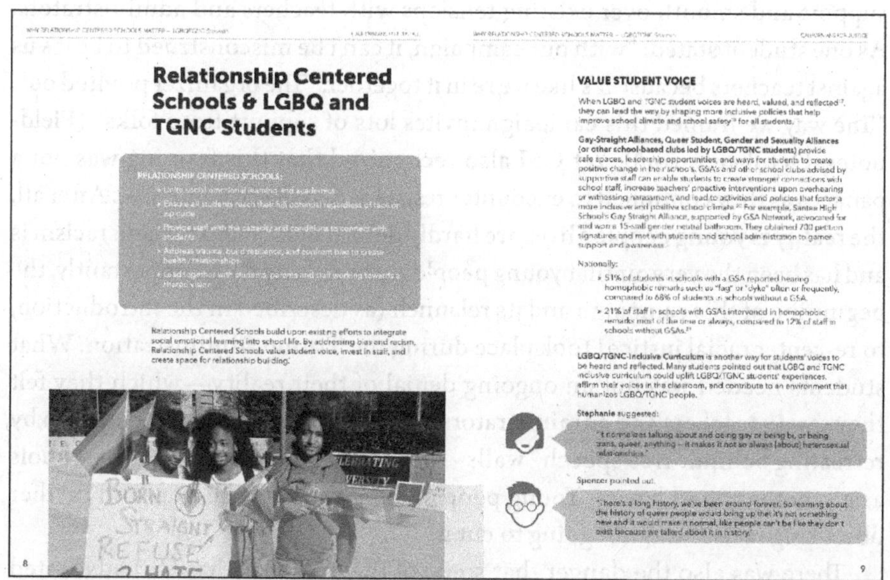

## Relationship Centered Schools & LGBQ and TGNC Students

RELATIONSHIP CENTERED SCHOOLS:

- Unite social emotional learning and academics
- Ensure all students reach their full potential regardless of race or zip code
- Provide staff with the capacity and conditions to connect with students
- Address trauma, build resilience, and confront bias to create healthy relationships
- Lead together with students, parents and staff working towards a shared vision

Relationship Centered Schools build upon existing efforts to integrate social emotional learning into school life. By addressing bias and racism, Relationship Centered Schools value student voice, invest in staff, and create space for relationship building.

8

**VALUE STUDENT VOICE**

When LGBQ and TGNC student voices are heard, valued, and reflected[17], they can lead the way by shaping more inclusive policies that help improve school climate and school safety[19] for all students.

**Gay-Straight Alliances, Queer Student, Gender and Sexuality Alliances (or other school-based clubs led by LGBQ/TGNC students)** provide safe spaces, leadership opportunities, and ways for students to create positive change in their schools. GSA's and other school clubs advised by supportive staff can enable students to create stronger connections with school staff, increase teachers' proactive interventions upon overhearing or witnessing harassment, and lead to activities and policies that foster a more inclusive and positive school climate.[20] For example, Santee High School's Gay Straight Alliance, supported by GSA Network, advocated for and won a 15-stall gender neutral bathroom. They obtained 700 petition signatures and met with students and school administration to garner support and awareness.

Nationally:

- 51% of students in schools with a GSA reported hearing homophobic remarks such as "fag" or "dyke" often or frequently, compared to 68% of students in schools without a GSA.
- 21% of staff in schools with GSAs intervened in homophobic remarks most of the time or always, compared to 12% of staff in schools without GSAs.[21]

**LGBQ/TGNC-Inclusive Curriculum** is another way for students' voices to be heard and reflected. Many students pointed out that LGBQ and TGNC inclusive curriculum could uplift LGBQ/TGNC students' experiences, affirm their voices in the classroom, and contribute to an environment that humanizes LGBQ/TGNC people.

**Stephanie** suggested:

"It normalizes talking about and being gay or being bi, or being trans, queer, anything – it makes it not so always [about] heterosexual relationships."

Spencer pointed out:

"There's a long history, we've been around forever. So learning about the history of queer people would bring up that it's not something new and it would make it normal, like people can't be like they don't exist because we talked about it in history."

9

One youth leader brought up a "Newcomers" club at their high school, where students welcome new immigrant students and act as leaders to engender a strong sense of belonging. Others shared stories of already translating for their friends or new immigrant students. Again, then, research uplifted how students of color are not just adults-in-waiting, but already transforming their environments for the better in ways that portend a bright possibility if their creativity and leadership were only fully invested in.

## Centering Race

Research supported the RCS campaign's efforts to unapologetically center both racism and racial justice. Like other racial justice organizations in a society bent simultaneously on reducing racism to individual pathology despite the dogged persistence of racial hostilities, CFJ has had to navigate a minefield wherein white teachers and administrators are more concerned about being called racist than disrupting racism. The initial messaging of the campaign thus highlighted the universal appeal of "relationships" to attract a broader base of support and smooth over existing tensions with teachers and administrators. As one student stated: "with our campaign, it can't be misconstrued to be it's us against teachers because it's like we're in it together." The organizer pointed out: "The way we framed this campaign invites lots of support from folks" (Fieldnotes, October 2, 2018). Yet CFJ also recognized that this framing was not a panacea as they continued to encounter resistance, as described above. After all, the reality is young people's lives are hardly devoid of race and racism: racism is and has been the very air that young people are breathing daily. Importantly, the beginning of this campaign and its relaunch (as described in the introduction, to re-center racial justice) took place during the Trump administration. What students needed was not an ongoing denial of their reality—which they felt they saw in teachers and administrators who dismissed emboldened racism by retreating behind "free speech" walls—but a full-throated embrace of schools as a sanctuary and haven. Young people's lives were on the line, and further obscuring racism was not going to cut it.

There was also the danger that some of the practices that CFJ advocated for—such as restorative justice and social emotional learning—were becoming another way to grease the wheels of white supremacy. As other scholars and educators have pointed out, such practices that do not explicitly engage with the context of systemic racism obscure and deepen structural inequalities. For example, asserting that young people should merely cultivate grit, resilience, or a set of social emotional skills to transcend their situations "place the onus of social and emotional health on the very young people whose social stressors have been shaped because of dispossession and marginalization" (Camangian & Cariaga, 2022, p. 3). As Ginwright (2015) points out: "social emotional practices rarely focus on building awareness, consciousness, and actions that address the social conditions that threaten social emotional health in the first place" (p. 8). Without explicit grounding as resistance to structural racism, this suite of practices can merely be weaponized in service of oppression.

CFJ, understandably, wanted to firmly root the RCS campaign around this more explicit critique of racism and vision of racial justice, and the research brief was an instrumental component. I collaborated with CFJ staff to address three main assumptions: namely, that racism is "too hard to change," that relationships have nothing to do with disrupting racism, and that education is not the focal point for addressing racism. The opening salvo of the brief, written by Saa'un P. Bell, highlighted this shift in messaging:

> Despite knowing the historic and current reality of how race has shaped our country and schools, as a state, we shy away from addressing race and racial inequality head-on. Instead, we choose to use catchalls like "low-income" & "high-needs" to address the persistent inequities in today's education system. **We need to center race in our words, in our actions, and in our policies to truly address the inequities students of color face in today's schools.** (*Why Race and Relationships Matter in California Schools*, 2018, p. 2)

This noticeable contrast to messaging that instead focused more broadly on caring teachers draws back the veil of race avoidance and argues against race eliding maneuvers. Such sentiments were also reflected in student speeches in Sacramento in May 2018, when Angelo argued: "Race is the most powerful determinant in students of color's lives. It's not separate from socioeconomic status, or gender. It's not something you can just check and leave at the door." CFJ youth leaders, in their organizing, then, grappled with the full gamut and complexities of race, refusing how educational researchers have referred to "race as a 'personal characteristic, literally reducing a system of domination to an individual trait" (Orum Hernández & Barcelos, 2023, p. 93).

In one sense, we did this by engaging vast and varied bodies of literature in the Race and Relationships brief—as depicted in Figure 6.1, threading connections of educational and racial justice with housing, immigration, and criminal justice. To combat historical amnesia and individualistic thinking, our English Learner brief highlighted how Proposition 227 essentially decimated bilingual education and fostered disengagement and psychological impacts like emotional distress, anxiety, depression, and school-phobia for English Learners. We also took pains to unravel commonly used narratives such as the "achievement gap," which focuses on disparities of educational attainment but can easily be deployed without context to fall back on regressive explanations that circulate around ostensible students of color's deficiency or cultures of poverty. Instead, we pointed out that

> "achievement gaps must be contextualized within the policies, practices, and perceptions that uphold systemic racism, including the **opportunity gap and belief gap**. The **opportunity gap** is seen in disparities in access to resources for educational success that map onto racial inequities, such as high-quality teachers, pre-K programs, college preparatory programs, civic learning, arts and music, and adequate facilities and technology." (*Why Race and Relationships Matter in California Schools*, 2018, p. 4)

The research brief ultimately attempted a monumental task of briefly cataloguing systemic racial inequities.

We also tackled how systemic racism can also be more subtle and hard to pinpoint. For example, our LGBQ/TGNC brief provided more intersectional, expansive understanding of safety to undo rather than fortify the nexus of racialized and gendered policing as targeting LGBQ/TGNC students of color. We were careful to situate our work in relationship to allies such as Gender and Sexualities Alliance Network as a broader project to refuse white "queer investments in punishment" (Lamble, 2013, p. 230), such as anti-bullying policies that expand the school to prison pipeline that redouble punishment for LGBQ/TGNC students of color (Orum Hernández & Barcelos, 2023). For example, we cited GSAN's research which found that LGBQ and TGNC students of color who attempt to protect themselves from bullying or report the issue to teachers are told that mistreatment is the result of their gender nonconforming behavior, and that TGNC and LGBQ youth of color receive harsher punishment than white students or peers who are not perceived as LGBQ/TGNC for the same infractions (Burdge, Hyemingway, & Licona, 2014a, 2014b).

Rather than fall into carceral traps, we worked with young people to critique systemic and intersecting contexts of racism, transphobia, homophobia, and gendered violence, and the harms caused by a situation where schools rely on punishment but have divested dramatically from relationship building. For example, students pointed out that discipline becomes the only tool that teachers can use—when students use homophobic or transphobic slurs, teachers punish them for infractions against school rules, but this does not automatically open a portal to learning or education. Our students also highlighted a common site of gender policing—both in the literal and more broad senses—in the lack of gender-neutral restrooms. Even if they do exist, youth pointed out that they can become sites of further policing by school resource officers. Ultimately, then, research provided a buttressing framework for uplifting racial and gender justice as intertwined and recognizing that the root causes must be addressed.

## Investing in Care

Finally, research uplifted how CFJ youth leaders' needs for caring relationships and meaningful connections with staff connect to demands for structural change. Our research echoed and informed campaign messaging around systemic racism as a root cause for why students of color often have less supportive relationships with teachers: for example, in the forces that converge to create a predominantly white teaching force and under-resourced schools that inhibit teachers' capacity to connect. While teachers still needed to be held accountable for punitive behavior that wrought real damaging consequences on students, organizers also tried to link teachers' behavior to their working and living conditions, in which students and teachers alike felt the walls closing in on them as they struggled to survive. For example, in a political education workshop where students highlighted dimensions of caring teachers, the organizer pointed out:

> But we all know teachers are not all super set up to do all the things we need them to. So we're asking people in power to invest in staff, to not just be these superheroes . . . So that's going to be a big part of our messaging, that all teachers have the support and investment to be really great. (Fieldnotes, February 16, 2019)

This messaging was reflected in the Race and Relationships brief, where we asserted that "shifting the culture and climate of schools requires us to address interpersonal racism by investing in our staff's capacity to deeply listen to students, to bravely talk about the impact of racism in our schools, and to boldly act by centering practices that build relationships based on mutual appreciation and accountability" (16). Our research highlighted how insufficient compensation and salary especially impact teachers of color and can deter them from teaching in the first place: for example, teachers with the least preparation are two to three times more likely to leave the profession or their positions: this disproportionately impacts teachers of color, who are more likely to enter teaching through alternative certification pathways (Carver-Thomas, 2018). Yet, it is immeasurably important for students to have teachers who resonate with their experiences and have the skills to connect. As Erica, CFJ youth leader, put it in our interview for the English Language Learner brief: "I wish I had more teachers that were bilingual who I could go to and ask for to help and not just have few options." Some of the teachers of color we spoke to in our baseline research echoed challenges. While many of them stepped up and filled a void in addressing racial disparities in school (for example, by initiating efforts to mentor Black students), they also experienced backlash and a lack of necessary support.

Research on teacher challenges, then, helped to further form coalitions and emphasized that if we want teachers to care for students, then we need to care for them, beyond empty accolades and through actual investments. The Oakland chapter's action research supported organizing demands for investing in staff. The report highlighted systemic conditions behind teacher attrition, such as meager salaries and benefits in light of the astronomical cost of living in the Bay Area. Those who stayed coped by commuting or crowded living situations. One teacher shared: "I got priced out of Oakland and now I commute. That's an hour longer to my day just to work for OUSD." This finding was corroborated by Oakland Unified's own exit survey, which found that 67% of teachers who left their positions in OUSD did so because of low salaries (Harrington, 2019). And disinvestment also fostered working conditions that only layered on the indignities. As one teacher noted, "I have ants for months in my classroom, where temperatures reach 90 degrees 40–60 days each year." Teachers also spoke to excessive work pressures and stresses, including high stakes testing. Again, teachers' living and working conditions deeply impact how students learn. As Jiawen, CFJ student leader wrote in the brief:

> When teachers come and go, we lose the strong connections students need to feel safe and comfortable at school. We can struggle and fall behind in our classes. We can become overwhelmed and not know who to turn to for assistance. We can check out and go through an

> entire day without talking in class or connecting with an adult. (*Relationship Centered Schools: Teacher Retention Starts with Relationships, 2018, p. 4*)

At the same time, CFJ's teacher survey found that that although 70% of teachers believe meaningful relationships are a priority, far less (39%) believed that their school provides them with support to foster those meaningful relationships—such as professional development, mentoring, and time. In our baseline research interviews, teachers told me that they had not been encouraged nor supported in their teacher training to develop relationships with students or to cultivate a race and class consciousness. One teacher told me that she was originally very strict with students and unforgiving. It wasn't until she once visited a student—her first time ever seeing the projects—that she realized that she needed to treat them with compassion for systemic racism, poverty, and trauma. Another teacher told me that he only by chance happened upon books that made him more aware of race and class differences and the need to develop good relationships with his students during his struggles as a new teacher. As he pointed out, his approach of caring relationships and racial/class consciousness was not something that was encouraged by the district, nor the school. In fact, master teachers encouraged him to be even more strict. That such teachers happened upon their critical consciousness and empathy for students by accident demonstrates a systemic failure in teacher training.

However, research, in tandem with other aspects of CFJ's organizing, highlighted success stories of caring teachers that modeled the type of radical love, care, and abundance that youth of color so deeply deserve. For example, CFJ youth leaders who are English Learner students also shared the specific importance of supportive teachers, especially those who also came from immigrant backgrounds. Youth leader Viri also reflected on the influence of a teacher who buoyed her esteem when she had qualms about her English ability, encouraging her to challenge herself when she didn't believe in her own potential: "She said you should take AP English Language. And I said no, English is my second language, I cannot do it. And she said, do it. So now I'm doing it. She's really supportive and if it wasn't for her I wouldn't be taking this class right now." This teacher also shared her own experiences of being an immigrant from the

Philippines as a teenager. As Viri reflected in her interview conducted for the English Learner brief:

> That was good because I felt that connection, we had this thing in common. She came at 15, I came at 15. I felt closer to her. She's one of my favorite teachers, and I still talk to her . . . If a teacher understands your story or your past or your struggle it's gonna be easier for them to understand you.

Viri's story reflects that of countless others that CFJ collected, of teachers who went above and beyond to check in, believe in, and care for students, and the particular importance of teachers who could meaningfully connect with students based on similar experiences. Together, these cases were glimmers of hope, a rupture in the everyday fabric of racism that erodes connection and relationships. By forging these relationships, teachers and students alike showed the possibility of what could be.

But, again, the burden should not be on teachers to go above and beyond. The problem is systemic, and through research and organizing, CFJ has been pushing for institutional changes such as master schedule changes, common prep time, advisories, and paid time for teachers outside of school hours. As a teacher participant in CFJ's focus group explained: "I think a whole lot more of relationship building would happen if teachers had more time. We should have a prep every single day." Of course, this has also involved supporting teachers' strikes for equitable compensation, as well as high quality and affordable entry and retention pathways to support more teachers of color in the workforce. Ultimately, as we concluded, the vision of Relationship Centered Schools is one where "teachers have the resources and support they need to make schools an inclusive place that embraces, encourages, and empowers students of color to pursue their dreams" (Why Race and Relationships Matter in California's Schools, 2018). In other words, we need school conditions that humanize and deeply care for all school staff and students alike.

## Conclusion

Research is merely one tool in the vast strategies wielded by community organizing and movement building—all of which are needed to undo the daunting landscape of power and all its machinations. In this chapter, I have highlighted how research can be used to uplift other strategies of youth organizing, from centering the voice and decisions of students of color most impacted by racial, educational, and intersectional injustices, to bolstering narrative change that firmly grounds campaigns in racial justice. Altogether, CFJ's organizing and research worked towards love in action and embraced young people's possibilities, pointing to abundance and models of student leadership rather than scarcity as foregone conclusion. Key to their transformative work is not just the idea that students of color should have a few seats at the table, but that the idea of the table, like schools, must be dramatically re-envisioned. Research can support how youth organizing spurs tectonic shifts in perceptions of young people and the valuing of student voices to identify school problems and forge creative solutions beyond the reaches of limited adult imaginations. More than just a doom and gloom narrative, youth organizing is about possibility and hope. As staff wrote in the race and relationships brief:

> The 4.5 million students of color in California are calling on us to reimagine schools—to transform the institutional racism that is inherent in a factory model of education which deprioritizes the social and emotional development and unique needs and interests of students of color. Students call on us to create schools where every single young person feels like they belong and are safe and supported to succeed. (17)

Research thus supports youth organizing to dream and bring to fruition expansive visions of care that are not wholly defined by oppression, but rather unapologetically uplift youth of color enactments of deep care.

## End Note

1. Enacted in 2013, LCFF replaced the previous K-12 finance system in California. Under this new system, funding goes to districts based on student attendance. Districts receive additional funding based on numbers and concentration of "high-need" students: that is, low-income, English language learner, or foster youth. This means districts with more high-need students receive more funding than districts of comparable sizes with less high-need students. Additionally, districts are expected to outline how they use these additional funds through a Local Control Accountability Plan (LCAP).

## References

Burdge, H., Hyemingway, Z., & Licona, A. (2014a). *Gender nonconforming youth: Discipline disparities, school push-out, and the school to prison pipeline.* GSA Network and Crossroads Collaborative at the University of Arizona. https://gsanetwork.org/files/aboutus/GSA_GNC_FINAL-web.pdf

Burdge, H., Hyemingway, Z., & Licona, A. (2014b). *LGBTQ youth of color: Discipline disparities, school push-out, and the school to prison pipeline.* GSA Network and Crossroads Collaborative at the University of Arizona. https://gsanetwork.org/files/aboutus/GSA_GNC_FINAL-web.pdf

Camangian, P., & Cariaga, S. (2022). Social and emotional learning is hegemonic miseducation: Students deserve humanization instead. *Race Ethnicity and Education, 25*(7), 901–921. https://doi.org/10.1080/13613324.2020.1798374

Carver-Thomas, D. (2018). *Diversifying the teaching profession through high-retention pathways.* Learning Policy Institute. https://learningpolicyinstitute.org/product/diversifying-teaching-profession-brief

Esqueda, H. (2023, June 27). Celebrating 3 years of school transformation in Long Beach. *Californians for Justice.* https://caljustice.org/2023/06/27/celebrating-3-years-of-school-transformation-in-long-beach/

Ginwright, S. (2015). *Hope and healing in urban education: How urban activists and teachers are reclaiming matters of the heart.* Routledge.

Harrington, T. (2019, January). *Oakland Unified looks to higher teacher pay to improve student learning as teachers threaten to strike.* EdSource. https://edsource.org/2019/as-teachers-threaten-to-strike-oakland-unified-looks-to-higher-teacher-pay-to-improve-student-learning/606381

HoSang, D. M. (2010). *Racial propositions: Ballot initiatives and the making of postwar California.* University of California Press.

Ignacio, P. (2022, April 27). 26 moments from 26 years of CFJ. *Californians for Justice*. https://caljustice.org/2022/04/27/26-moments-with-cfj/

Lamble, S. (2013). Queer necropolitics and the expanding carceral state: Interrogating sexual investments in punishment. *Law and Critique, 24*(3), 229–253. https://doi.org/10.1007/s10978-013-9125-1

Orum Hernández, G., & Barcelos, C. (2023). Queer punishments: School safety and youth of color in the United States. *Equity & Excellence in Education, 56*(1–2), 87–99. https://doi.org/10.1080/10665684.2022.2159897

Pastor, M. (2018). *State of resistance: What California's dizzying descent and remarkable resurgence mean for America's future*. The New Press.

"Relationship centered schools programs and practices." (n.d.). Californians for Justice. https://drive.google.com/file/d/1jo5deJMWYKsEgF5jNuk9vYW23e4WCCop/view

*Relationship centered schools: Teacher retention starts with relationships*. (2018). Californians for Justice. https://mayhlin.com/wp-content/uploads/2018/07/v4-full-spread-RCS-Oakland-Teacher-Shortage-Report.pdf

Serrano, U., Turner, D. C., Regalado, G., & Banuelos, A. (2022). Towards community rooted research and praxis: Reflections on the BSS safety and youth justice project. *Social Sciences, 11*(5), Article 5. https://doi.org/10.3390/socsci11050195

Staley, S. (2018). On getting stuck: Negotiating stuck places in and beyond gender and sexual diversity-focused educational research. *Harvard Educational Review, 88*(3), 287–307. https://doi.org/10.17763/1943-5045-88.3.287

Terriquez, V. (2017). *Building healthy communities through youth leadership: The comprehensive developmental outcomes of youth organizing*. USC Program for Environmental and Regional Equity. https://dornsife.usc.edu/assets/sites/242/docs/BHC_YouthOrganizing_2pgr_August2017.pdf

Terriquez, V., & Lin, M. (2016). *Californians for Justice; Supporting the leadership and healthy development of youth in Fresno, Long Beach, Oakland, and San Jose*. USC Program for Environmental and Regional Equity. https://dornsife.usc.edu/assets/sites/242/docs/VT_CFJ_Report.2016.pdf

*Why race and relationships matter in California schools*. (2018). Californians for Justice. https://caljustice.egnyte.com/dl/XDr3C96lKt

*Why relationship centered schools matter for lesbian, gay, bisexual, queer/transgender and gender non-conforming students*. (2018). Californians for Justice. https://caljustice.org/resource/why-relationship-centered-schools-matter-for-lesbian-gay-bisexual-queer-transgender-and-gender-non-conforming-students/

# Section III

# Policy and/or Networking as Justice Work

## Chapter 7

# Indigenous Approaches to Equity Research: A Story of California's Central Coast Community

*Morgan Love (Tlingit), Kathleen Knight, Jonnie Williams (Diné), and Marcos Vargas (Chicano Sundancer in the Lakota Tradition)*

## Our Community

We are living in a time of unparalleled challenge on California's Central Coast—made up of Santa Barbara, San Luis Obispo, and Ventura Counties—as we grapple with the still unfolding consequences of the COVID-19 pandemic, structurally embedded patterns and practices of systemic racism, and the immediately clear and present dangers of human-induced climate change. It is also a time to reassess and reorder our priorities in light of the long-standing inequities this confluence of challenges has brought so starkly into view. We, on California's Central Coast, have certainly not been spared from the devastating impact of these calamities and must heed the call to take action. We have experienced our share of climate disasters, the legacy of racism, and the devastating human impact of the pandemic. While the region's prosperous economy, based in large part on thriving tourism, agriculture, and growing technology sectors, has benefited many of our residents, many more have been left behind—struggling without a living-wage job, affordable housing, or basic health care.

The Central Coast region faces a multi-dimensional crisis of inequality that manifests in wages and employment, housing, criminal justice, education, environmental exposures, and access to health care. This crisis weighs most heavily on working-class communities of color. The depth and extent of these inequities were brought to the surface by the devastating, racially disparate impacts of the COVID-19 pandemic, but they are rooted in structural trends, policies, and practices that have been shaping regional fortunes for decades (O'Connor et al., 2021). With this growing emphasis on structural inequities across the region, the Central Coast Regional Equity Initiative[1] (CCREI) formed as a collaborative movement that aims to advocate for social, health, environmental, and economic equity through region-wide cross-sector collaboration, community and research-informed action, and an indigenized and decolonized approach.

Community voice has informed all aspects of our evaluation and planning, from the data collection and rigorous scientific analysis for the CCREI's first report entitled "Towards a Just and Equitable Central Coast,"[2] to collaborative learning opportunities to move the CCREI forward, and actionizing data through a community-led Strategic Action Plan. We define "community-led" as an evaluation and planning process that centers community perspectives at a foundational level and leverages scientific models to support community knowledge base building through:

- helping community frame questions
- providing research path options
- consistently seeking community feedback with a willingness to adapt methodologies
- engaging community wisdom in the analysis process
- promoting collective community ownership of the body of work.

Engagement in true community-led evaluation and planning contributes to a greater readiness for cross-sector collaborative action, a sense of community ownership over solutions to equity issues, and sets the stage for deeper rooted, long-term success. Guided by an Indigenous worldview-informed vision rooted in equity, sustainability, and justice, we offer this chapter as an example of successful community-led evaluation and planning that supports equity-centered action organizing around the region's racial, economic, environmental, and political inequities.

## Our Team

Our evaluation and planning team included staff members from The Fund for Santa Barbara and Evolve Equity. Both organizations are deeply committed to systems change work, and support community-led approaches to social justice and equity.

Evolve Equity advances health equity, racial justice, and systems change through indigenous worldview and scientific practices for groups that have been historically, socially, and economically marginalized. Evolve Equity provides research, evaluation, and training services to government agencies, corporations, philanthropic organizations, tribal nations, and nonprofits. Dr. Jonnie Williams (Diné) and Morgan Love (Tlingit) are proud Native researchers who strive to decolonize research methods using Indigenous worldview to inform research practices, standards, and protocols by maintaining ethical practices from a trauma-informed and community-based participatory research approach.

The Fund for Santa Barbara advances progressive change by strengthening movements for Economic, Environmental, Political, Racial, and Social Justice. The Fund for Santa Barbara is a nontraditional community foundation that supports organizations and groups working for progressive social change in California's Central Coast. Dr. Marcos Vargas (Chicano Sundancer in the Lakota Tradition) and Kathleen Knight are community members who serve as regional intermediaries between Central Coast grassroots organizations and the region's philanthropic, policy, and research communities through deep relational and justice-centered practices.

Through this collaborative partnership, our diverse experiences, stories, and expertise contribute to a synergistic team committed to co-creating new approaches to community empowerment.

## Indigenous Approach

It is important to recognize that knowledge systems of Indigenous peoples vary throughout the world. In this chapter, we have integrated values from the Chumash peoples of our local region, a Diné worldview, and elements from the Gathering of Native Americans curriculum (King & Guillory, 2015). Our work, which takes place in California's Central Coast on unceded Chumash and Tataviam lands, relies on an Indigenous worldview and knowledge systems as we commit to respecting the rights and experiences of Indigenous peoples, both of this land and all others.

The Central Coast has a long and growing history of interconnectedness that reaches beyond economies and history of regional activism—a history that is rooted in the genocide and colonization of the Chumash and Tataviam peoples. The story of our region begins with the region's first people—the Native Chumash. Archaeological and anthropological studies document their inhabitance dating back over 13,000 years, where, prior to European occupation, as many as 20,000 Chumash lived from Southern Ventura County north to San Luis Obispo County. The region also includes the ancestral land of the Tataviam people, who inhabited a small portion of southern Ventura County and northwest Los Angeles County. During the Spanish invasion and colonial settlement of California in the late eighteenth century (c. 1769–1833), the Spanish-imposed mission system deployed violence, genocide, slavery, and forced relocation as well as the cultural suppression associated with religious conversion against the Indigenous people of the California Central Coast, including the Chumash (O'Connor et al., 2021).

The continued existence of the Chumash people today can be in large part attributed to their many well documented acts of organized resistance and their resilient cultural adaptations. Chumash leaders and grassroots activists today continue to engage in actions of cultural self-determination and the protection of their ancestral land. The Central Coast has been and remains to this day Indigenous land, with the Chumash people serving as its original caretakers. The Chumash people remain central to the history and future of the Central Coast (O'Connor et al., 2021).

Colonization actively continues in the present day through continued Indigenous struggles for political rights, cultural recognition, and land protection, thus contributing to a continued erasure of Indigenous ways of life and perpetuation of inequities that significantly harm our region's Indigenous peoples. The first principle and priority that guides the Central Coast Regional Equity Initiative's equity work is to "respect the rights and experiences of Indigenous peoples," and in this spirit, we integrated an Indigenized approach to data collection processes and action planning by interweaving traditional values. Our equity work is grounded in an Indigenous approach, drawing upon Indigenous values and nature-based metaphors reflective of the region's physical environment to begin addressing inequities in the social environment. The following values shaped our community-led evaluation and planning approach, and include:

- **Interdependence with the Natural World.** Creating an empowered community requires respect and harmony with the natural world (Wilson, 2008). The world in which we live, we are borrowing from future generations. Healing is created through harmonious and balanced relationships with the environment, intergenerationally, and in community (Fast & Kovach, 2019; Shirley & Angulo, 2019).
- **Cultural Identity and Humility.** The practice of cultural humility guides social change through authentic and respectful relationships with others. Awareness of one's own cultural context and intersectional identities is necessary for forming authentic relationships, especially as worldviews are rooted in knowledge, personal life experiences, and interactions with others across their ecological contexts (Clauss-Ehlers et al., 2019). To create an authentic, empowered community, cultural humility and recognition of intersectional identities within social, political, and economic systems is a foundational practice (Hearst & Dutton, 2021).
- **Reciprocity.** Defined as mutualistic giving and receiving within all relationships that enables continued growth, encourages generosity, and balances responsibility (Kuokkanen, 2007; Wilson, 2008). Creating an empowered community based on reciprocity fosters mutual respect and interconnection, foundational for collective action (Fast & Kovach, 2019).
- **Storytelling Methods.** Stories are an Indigenous way of teaching, learning, and knowing. By using story, we acknowledge that we are in process and co-creating a narrative with intention for the context with which the story is shared (Archibald,

2008). Stories are a method of motivating and guiding action and processing shared experience.
- **Decolonization and Restorative Justice.** Decolonization is both a goal and systemic institutional change process to bring about a fundamental shift in colonial structures, ideologies, and resources (Monchalin, 2016). It is an anti-colonial struggle of recovery and healing that grows out of grassroots spaces, meaningful alliances, and social justice (Zavala, 2013; Tuck & Yang, 2012).

In addition to these guiding values, our team integrated additional values from the Gathering of Native Americans (GONA) curriculum, which are rooted in human growth and healing that are found in Native cultures (King & Guillory, 2015). Two elements that we will share in this chapter include:

- **Belonging.** A place for all ages. A place for all kinds of people. Represents infancy and childhood, a time when we need to know how we belong.
- **Mastery.** Empowerment, for individuals, and for the community. Honors adolescence as a time of vision and mastery (King & Guillory, 2015).

As explained by researcher George J. Sefa Dei, Indigenous research is rooted in a diverse Indigenous values system that bring with them their own unique methodological and theoretical framework, accepted by an epistemic community of Indigenous peoples, and not only "certified" Indigenous scholars (2013). We challenge Western research practices by sharing an example of a community-led evaluation and planning process, and how community's continuous engagement, feedback, and analysis are the results, rather than it being a small part of the researchers' analyses or a "checking off a box." In other words, Indigenous research foregrounds local community members' voices in research, rather than subordinating their contributions to the researcher's analysis and the literature (Sefa Dei, 2013). Our exploration of Indigenous values-driven research models as alternatives to standard Western research science practices are not only valid alternatives to the standard research continuum, but they can actually be a much better fit for deep rooted community work as Indigenous research integrates a much more holistic approach.

In this chapter, we share stories that demonstrate how dynamic research-based community action and organizing truly are. Although the story of the Central Coast community is growing and evolving, this chapter will focus on evaluation, planning, wisdom sharing, and collaboration—and showcase how community members are legitimate co-producers of knowledge and co-creators of equity solutions throughout the research continuum.

## Methods

We share this table of methods (Table 7.1), which details the methodologies used throughout our evaluation and planning process, including timelines, descriptions of the methods, and the corresponding Indigenous values reflected in the methods.

**Table 7.1:** Methods Summary Central Coast Initiative

| Method | Timeframe | Description | Indigenous Value(s) |
|---|---|---|---|
| Community Consultations | April 2020–March 2021 | Facilitators from The Fund for Santa Barbara and University of California Santa Barbara Blum Center on Poverty, Inequality, and Democracy facilitated sixteen 1.5–2 hour Community Consultations with over 160 community members, which all took place via Zoom. The consultations spanned eight general sessions and eight issue-specific sessions covering K-12 Education, Public Higher Education, Racial Justice, Housing & Houselessness, Access to Public Health, Small Business, Climate Justice, and finally, Criminal Justice and Reimagining Community Safety. Community members were asked some or all of the following questions:<br>• *How has the pandemic affected your work?*<br>• *What information in our Equity Study would be helpful in your work?*<br>• *What are the highest priority issues for you?* | Cultural Identity & Humility<br>Storytelling Methods<br>Decolonization & Restorative Justice |

| Method | Timeframe | Description | Indigenous Value(s) |
|---|---|---|---|
| Report Launch | December 2021 | The report launch was facilitated by The Fund, UCSB Blum Center, USC Equity Research Institute, and included perspectives of support from local policy leaders and community organizations. We shared data, key insights, and the Principles and Priorities from the report to an in-person audience of 80 and a virtual audience of 150. | Storytelling Methods |
| Engagement Events | January 2022– August 2023 | We shared data and key report findings, as well as the equity-centered action organizing framework for the Central Coast Regional Equity Initiative in conversations with change-oriented community groups, including:<br>• The Fund's Lunchtime Activist Network (January 2022)<br>• Central Coast Regional Capacity Building Collaborative (February 2023)<br>• The Fund's Board of Directors and community-led Grant Making Committee (March 2023)<br>• Policymakers and Philanthropic Leaders Briefing (April 2022)<br>• UCSB Blum Center Community-Engaged Research RFP (April 2022)<br>• UCSB Blum Center's Housing Forums (April and May 2022)<br>• Working Together for Transformative Change with Nonprofit Resource Network (May 2022)<br>• Central Coast Immigration Network (May 2022)<br>• Alliance for Community Transformation (June 2022)<br>• Southern California Association of Governments (June 2022)<br>• Working Together for Transformative Change with Nonprofit Resource Network Part 2 (August 2022)<br>• Partnership for Excellence (October 2022)<br>• UC Santa Cruz All-In: Co-Creating Knowledge for Justice conference (October 2022) | Cultural Identity & Humility<br>Storytelling Methods<br>Reciprocity<br>Decolonization & Restorative Justice |

| Method | Timeframe | Description | Indigenous Value(s) |
|---|---|---|---|
| Materials/ Tool Production | February 2022– January 2023 | Our team has created a variety of free, open-access resources for community activists, local political leaders, researchers, and philanthropic partners to use, which include:<br>• The Initiative's first website, www.centralcoastequity.org<br>• The "Executive Summary" and "Resumen Ejecutivo," which provide an insight into key inequities from the full report and help advance language justice and inclusivity in resource/information access<br>• Community Consultations Report, which provides practical insight and a framework tool for conducting community-led research<br>• A resource library of nine issue-area specific mini-reports, to make the data from the full report more easily accessible and serve as tools for community groups<br>• A collection of issue-area infographics, which provide visuals and text that can be posted to social media to circulate information on inequity<br>• A growing online resource library, which provides links to the data sources used for the report and additional equity tools<br>• Recordings of various community engagement events, which provide context to the CCREI and in-depth, meaningful discussions with community members | Reciprocity<br>Decolonization & Restorative Justice<br>Mastery |
| Strategic Action Plan: Workgroup 1 Meeting | August 2022 | The Fund and Evolve Equity facilitated a Workgroup meeting with 23 Community Leaders who represent 6 sectors (Philanthropic Funders Sector; Research Sector; Business Sector; Policy Maker Sector; Community-Based Organizations, Nonprofit Organizations, and Direct Service Providers Sector; and Policy Advocacy and Organizing Sector) and span over 3 counties (Santa Barbara, Ventura, San Luis Obispo) to discuss cross-sector collaborative action. 17 out of 23 leaders attended (Evolve Equity, 2023) | Belonging |
| Strategic Action Plan: Individual Interviews | September 2022 | 22 out of the 23 Community Leaders participated in the interviews. The 30 minute interviews took place virtually and thematic coding analysis was conducted based on the phases of collaborative action. | Belonging<br>Mastery<br>Reciprocity |

## The Wisdom of Experience

A core component of the evaluation and planning process for the Central Coast Regional Equity Initiative's first report, *Towards a Just and Equitable Central Coast,* centered on Community Consultations to understand community members' lived experiences of inequities with the intention of co-creating a research narrative on equity in the region. The Community Consultations were a space for community members and facilitators to imagine and motivate change, informed by data, and create shared ideas about how to guide action toward a more equitable future. Communal wisdom shared during the Community Consultations informed the tone and directionality of the report, including the issue areas highlighted in the report and the frameworks for social change and action. These discussions also served as a way for processing shared experience, as community members explored how the murders of George Floyd and Breonna Taylor and the experience of the COVID-19 pandemic had exacerbated or otherwise brought existing inequities to light.

Reflecting Indigenous values of Storytelling Methods and Cultural Identity & Humility, community members (including local activists, and regional leaders) shared their unique and nuanced experiences with inequities in conversations around how inequities are experienced and perceived by the people who work, live, learn, and participate in civic life in the Central Coast. Community members' insights reflected diverse perspectives and blended both personal and professional reflections on barriers to equity in California's Central Coast. Also reflecting Cultural Identity & Humility, the facilitated spaces acknowledged and respected the intersectional identities unique to each participant, contributing to building an empowered community in which individuals felt comfortable and respected when sharing their stories and experiences. In the wake of George Floyd and Breonna Taylor's murders, our community spent significant time processing, sharing, and healing during the Racial Justice Community Consultation. The Indigenous value of Decolonization & Restorative Justice was vitally important in informing a safe and trusting space as community members discussed impacts of racism within our local governments and health care agencies, research and education institutions, and within our social community. Multiple community members shared a deep understanding of the intersection of race and inequities, elevating that Black, Indigenous, and People of Color frequently experienced inequities widely across the board. Community members specifically asked for data that elevated these disparities along racial demographic lines and across a variety of areas where inequity was felt, including housing, language justice, and medical access and also shared ideas for integrated and coordinated approaches to racial justice.

These discussions at the Community Consultations significantly informed the framework and data in *Towards a Just and Equitable Central Coast* and contributed to a deeper understanding of just how nuanced and intersectional existing inequities are experienced by community members—particularly community members of color and marginalized groups. This led the evaluation and planning team to explore data in a more meaningful way, moving beyond surface level data and into intersectional approaches and analyses to better understand a fuller picture of inequity in the Central Coast. Methodologies combined both these qualitative data from the Community Consultations and quantitative analysis of U.S. Census data and was conducted in co-partnership with The Fund for Santa Barbara, University of California Santa Barbara (UCSB) Blum Center on Poverty, Inequality, and Democracy and the University of Southern California (USC) Equity Research Institute.

Understanding the social, economic, political, and environmental history of our region contributes to a deeper understanding of existing inequities, as well as serves as an offering to help inform addressing these inequities moving forward. We never intended *Towards a Just and Equitable Future* to be another report that sat on the shelf, but rather serve as a starting point for discussion and action around addressing the deep inequities in the Central Coast. We recognize that the road to equity is long—and must include a deep understanding of the intersectionality of issues, policies, and practices that have shaped our region for decades. The CCREI speaks to the urgent need for collective action that draws on the resources of local government, philanthropy, businesses, and academics as well as community activists and social movements.

*Towards a Just and Equitable Central Coast* not only shares a wealth of open-access intersectional data, but also amplifies this data through a call to action for a fundamental shift in colonial structures, ideologies, and resources. Our 11 Principles and Priorities for Research and Action offer guideposts for the region's equity work and inform the equity-centered action organizing strategies that drive the Central Coast Regional Equity Initiative. These Principles and Priorities frame the report in an intersectional way, speak to all of the issue areas of inequities shared in the report, and were co-developed by community liaisons from The Fund for Santa Barbara and researchers from the UCSB Blum Center. They are a reflection of the Community Consultation discussions and the intersectionality of the equity report.

The Principles and Priorities include:

1. Respect the rights and experiences of Indigenous people
2. Center equity and justice as foundational economic values
3. Invest in inclusive, universally accessible infrastructures of opportunity and social provision
4. Advance racial and intersectional justice
5. Recognize, respect, and protect immigrant rights, civic integration, and political voice
6. Protect tenants, preserve communities, and make housing affordable for all
7. Be a leader in environmental and climate justice
8. Bridge digital divides for underserved communities
9. Create platforms for collaborative, community-engaged equity research
10. Build from our victories
11. Open avenues to participatory democracy

These Principles and Priorities elevate a way forward for a transition to a just and equitable future on the Central Coast, one that acknowledges a sense of shared fate and common purposes required for an effective response to addressing inequities. These Principles and Priorities inform the framework for the CCREI, which strategizes for addressing historical harms of colonization through marginalized communities re-taking social, economic, and political power. We made the first call to action at the Central Coast Regional Equity Study Launch event, through conversation engagement around key issues, data, and frameworks from the *Towards a Just and Equitable Central Coast* report. Through Storytelling Methods, we shared findings from the report and facilitated a panel discussion among report production leaders from The Fund for Santa Barbara, UCSB Blum Center on Poverty, Inequality, and Democracy, and the USC Equity Research Institute and a variety of community partners, including local policy leaders, community organizations, grassroots activists, and Central Coast community members.

Following the report launch, our collaborative team engaged in community discussions intended to weave together various sectors and facilitate conversations centered on collective action movement building, leveraging The Fund for Santa Barbara's robust Capacity Building Program to facilitate events and convene community members. We facilitated many community conversations, from briefings with regional policymakers and philanthropic leaders, to community wisdom sharing conversations around how organizations are leveraging the Initiative's frameworks and data. These gatherings have been wide-ranging, from intimate presentations to small community groups to large community events with entire sectors, and all leaned on Cultural Identity & Humility to help guide safe and inclusive spaces, regardless of gathering size and diversity. These discussions were sometimes broad overviews of the data from the report and the frameworks for change, and sometimes issue-area specific—such as discussions centered around the region's housing crisis and immigration reform. Each engagement event emphasized Storytelling and acknowledged the ongoing process of co-creating a narrative with intention for the context with which the story is shared. All events featured information from the report time for both facilitated and free-flowing discussions for community members to share their reactions, their experiences with inequities, and their wisdom for moving community-led solutions forward. This process of teaching, learning, and knowing occurred in Reciprocity, as community conversations around the report were intentional in providing opportunities for both our team to share our story of equity on the Central Coast and opportunities for community members to share their understandings of inequities and their visions for addressing equity issues.

Our three-part series, "Working Together for Transformative Change," hosted in partnership with local support organization Nonprofit Resource Network, deeply engaged local community organizations in the Central Coast Regional Equity Initiative. This series centered on building community consciousness and engagement with the Initiative, first sharing data from the report and open discussion time; elevating community groups who had already begun to use the equity data from *Towards a Just and Equitable Future* to do community organizing, leverage funding, and inform program development; and then culminating in a sector-wide 3-hour conversation on advancing equity in the Central Coast at the Partnership for Excellence event and providing community insight into our Strategic Action Planning process.

We also approached this community work with emphasis on Decolonization and Racial Justice, centering discussion spaces around change activation that acknowledged the impacts of colonization and manifestation of racial injustice and systemic inequities in leading regional institutions, including local government and higher education systems. Part of this decolonization work includes an intersectoral approach to build foundations for trust and cross-sector collaboration. This was evident in our engagement of high-level policymakers, key Santa Barbara and Ventura Counties staff members, and staff members and directors from regional grantmaking and philanthropic organizations—opening up the conversation across sectors to discuss more intentional efforts for interconnected change.

In the spirit of the Central Coast Regional Equity Initiative's tenth Principle and Priority to "build from our victories," we elevate that this collective "our" speaks to the community power that strengthens our region and our struggle for equity. Our collective success so far couldn't have happened without the broad community support we've received for the CCREI from the philanthropic sector, government, community-based organizations and leaders, and other researchers. As a community, we've been exploring how to advance equity in our region, empower community organizations to leverage data to strengthen their work, and build a community consciousness around the crisis of inequity in the Central Coast. This Initiative is a reflection of all of us—and our aspirations for an equitable future. While in the process of building the CCREI in 2022, we recognized the need for a process of ongoing community engagement and organizing grounded in a unified equity agenda and a clearer equity framework, and thus engaged in a community-led Strategic Action Plan to help inform the work in our community over the next 3 years and set the foundations for work well into the future.

## Empowering Community Action

To transform the data from the *Towards a Just and Equitable Central Coast* report into community-organized action, our team initiated our 3-year Strategic Action Planning (SAP) process in Fall 2022. By gathering 23 leaders who understand and reflect the Central Coast community, the SAP process was filled with diverse professions/roles, expertise, lived experiences, and perspectives. With this, centering all of those elements into a collective narrative for the CCREI was not an easy nor quick task to complete. We used a holistic, mixed-methods approach, and the data shared here stems from our first workgroup meeting and individual interviews. The entire SAP process interwove the Indigenous values of Belonging, Mastery, and Reciprocity. Indigenous methodologies utilize the power of qualitative data by using a whole-person lens, captured through storytelling and mixed method approaches. Cross-sector collaborative frameworks also advocate for a variety of research designs and the use of both quantitative and qualitative methods (Bryson et al., 2015).

Our team strove to hold space for these diverse perspectives and engage community leaders in strategic discussion. It started with grounding everyone in an open, safe space and with each other—and this is where the focus shifted from specific strategizing of the *Towards a Just and Equitable Central Coast* report data to how we were going to address inequities in our region together. Our first virtual workgroup meeting enabled 22 of the 23 community leaders to be in the same space for the first time, and with four breakout groups, common themes that arose were the need to acknowledge power imbalances and build trusting relationships in order to successfully engage in equity projects. There was general consensus that inequity issues are interconnected—therefore it made sense to address these issues collaboratively across sectors. Mixing and combining our expertise, roles, and lived experiences to actionize data and create long-lasting change is an amazing and ambitious idea, but our team still needed to facilitate discussions to figure out how to exactly do that.

After the first workgroup meeting, our team realized that we had crucial things to consider, particularly around better understanding cross-sector collaboration and what would make it successful. Community leaders shared their experience and perspectives on the power of long-term relationships; considering the CCREI's ambitious goals for equity-centered change, we also had to consider how to concurrently build trust to build sustainable relationships and effectively develop cohesive equity strategies. The challenge presented after this meeting was that we had to take a step back and set a collective vision, shared understanding, and create a willingness to connect on a deeper level. We were at first hesitant because while fostering safety and building relationships is important, other community leaders expressed that it would be too lengthy and not get us to building equity solutions fast enough. Our team had to sit with finding and implementing a balance. We had to build confidence in community leaders to trust our non-Western, Indigenous process and be willing to be open, transparent, and take healthy risks while simultaneously being respectful and kind to one another.

With these considerations, our team reframed all our initially planned interview questions and shifted focus to developing the four Phases of Collaborative Action, which include: 1) Building trusting cross-sector relationships; 2) Acknowledgment of power and privilege; 3) Successful reciprocal collaboration; and 4) Sustainable resource circulation (Evolve Equity, 2023). These four focus areas were developed from the insights, fears, strengths, hopes, and opportunities discussed in the first workgroup meeting and updated throughout the data collection process. We found it particularly remarkable that the responses from participants and the data collected paralleled Indigenous values of Belonging, Mastery, and Reciprocity.

Our evaluation and planning team first asked community leaders, "*What norms do you need to feel safe in the Initiative and collaborative relationships? What do trusting cross-sector relationships 'look like'?*" We asked this question not only in response to feedback from the first workgroup meeting, but to continue to ground the CCREI in a sense of belonging. We aimed to provide an opportunity for individual community leaders to have their contributions heard, valued, and respected, and establish a foundation for the duration of SAP process and beyond (King & Guillory, 2015). By establishing relationships between our team and community leaders, as well as between sectors, it makes trust-building a priority to ensure group safety, honesty, and integrity. This places emphasis on establishing true rapport with community leaders in order to generate meaningful data (Sefa Dei, 2013).

All community leaders shared various strengths around creating safety and form connections. They also expressed a need to establish collective norms and agreements, including mutual respect, listening, curiosity, understanding, safety, speaking openly and honestly, valuing each other, shared vision, and coming together. For example, one community leader shared:

> Mindset of "us" rather than "them." (Community Leader from Community-Based Organizations, Nonprofit Organizations, and Direct Service Providers Sector)

Most community leaders shared the importance of honoring each other's presence and the experience they bring to the space. This expands beyond people's job titles or the organization they represent, but also their life experiences, background, and individual skills. Therefore, role clarification and understanding are needed in the collective space to build trust. On the other hand, most community leaders explained that creating a trusting relationship takes time and how often in this type of work, the outcomes are the priority over the formation of authentic, long-term relationships. With this normalization, there is a hesitation to believe that the environment will be safe enough to raise legitimate fears, have real discussion, and be heard. Insight from community leaders highlighted how important trust is in these collaborative spaces and why we need to address inequity issues together:

> Essential to collaboration—how do we make decisions, resolve conflict, how do some of us step back or forward, share leadership, define success. (Community Leader from Community-Based Organizations, Nonprofit Organizations, and Direct Service Providers Sector)

Our team then asked community leaders, "*How do we acknowledge power imbalance and privilege?*" They expressed the need for it to be acknowledged, recognized and understood, as well as an understanding that those steps alone will not instantly resolve the existing power imbalance:

> Also very self aware that the relationship has not miraculously equalized simply because differences have been acknowledged. (Community Leader from Research Sector)

Not only was the question asked grounded in Mastery and an understanding of regional power imbalances, but community leaders demonstrated a clear response of Mastery in practice. Community leaders took time to share their understandings of historical trauma, and how these losses and grief undermine our wellness today and contribute to the inequitable systems we face. Additionally, in the spirit of the Indigenous value of Belonging, community leaders emphasized the importance of everyone both having a voice and being heard, as well as the importance of educating oneself on history and being open to continuous learning. Community leaders shared what makes Belonging successful:

> Raise up voices of those who aren't always heard, practicing and modeling this behavior. (Community Leader from Policy Maker Sector)

> Diverse experience, real time learning. (Community Leader from Community-Based Organizations, Nonprofit Organizations, and Direct Service Providers Sector)

Lastly, our team asked, *"What does a successful reciprocal collaboration look like to you? How do we successfully collaborate reciprocally, given power imbalances?"* Community leaders shared how in order to create successful collaborative projects, genuine reciprocity is needed to address equity issues and while in these settings, community leaders need to feel that their presence and expertise is valued in the space:

> Successful reciprocal collaboration requires a genuine regard—not just those who receive the benefits/receive the services—not just the recipients who are appreciative of what they are receiving; the agency/org providing that service is appreciative of how the service benefits them as well as the recipients. (Community Leader from Community-Based Organizations, Nonprofit Organizations, and Direct Service Providers Sector)

> Everyone recognizes how valuable everyone in the team is, and everyone has different strengths to contribute. (Community Leader from Research Sector)

Community leaders demonstrated an understanding and a practice of the Indigenous value of Reciprocity and reiterated the importance and need for the continuous cycle of giving and receiving. It is through reciprocity that successful collaboration is possible, which ultimately contributes to a more sustainable and resilient CCREI.

The findings from the individual interviews alone did not exactly outline a 3-year prescriptive plan of how to dismantle inequity systems and structures in the region—rather the results led to the development of feasible tools for successful community-led action, including CCREI norms and the 4 Phases Model for Collaborative Action (Evolve Equity, 2023) that empowers community leaders to work collaboratively on projects that specifically address inequity issues. In addition, the outcomes of these processes are under collective ownership, which challenges traditional research practices and the idea of intellectual property. Our goal is to encourage collective ownership and that knowledge should be shared to all people, which includes making it accessible. The Strategic Action Planning process gives us a common language framework and tools, which empowers the CCREI to advance equity from a deeply collaborative, intersectoral, and Indigenous perspective. Our community is currently leveraging the key strategies from the SAP to inform this collective equity work and continue to decolonize our region as we decolonize our perceptions of what research is.

## Towards a Just, Equitable, and Decolonized Future

Equity research, evaluation, and planning need to be designed for community, with community, and by community. Integrating traditional values is nothing new, but what is overdue is the need for it to be recognized and appreciated in the research and academic settings. Our Indigenous approach enabled a deeper understanding of the inequities we face along the Central Coast and contributed to a more meaningful body of work. This approach also led to more community engagement—ultimately laying foundations for community organizing and engagement moving forward much more effectively. While Indigenous research aims at transformation as an end goal (Sefa Dei, 2013), transformation is also in the process. An Indigenous research approach creates a "community of learners" among researchers and local community members in the research process, operating with shared responsibilities about the goal, purpose, ethics, and values of social research (Sefa Dei, 2013).

Integrating Indigenous values as a primary evaluation and planning framework is a way to actively decolonize the ways in which traditional Western research is conducted, and work to dismantle colonial systems of knowledge production. Indigenous research both seeks and strengthens relationships with our communities when searching for knowledge (Wilson, 2008) and ultimately is more reflective of community experience and wisdom as it better supports a deeper integration of research knowledge into community-led solutions. Research must honor a shared fate through co-creating community landscapes that are environmentally, economically, and politically interconnected and support equitable distribution of power and resources to empower communities to participate in decision-making that affects them.

Important to this work is honoring the time, voice, and energy that this type of knowledge co-creation takes and an understanding that this is not time-bound work—rather, this work is continually evolving... as are our communities! Community-led research, evaluation, and planning do not start and stop with engagement, but continue to uplift, engage, and empower community voices. Additionally, social change and progress can be extremely difficult to measure when using Western standards. Western models of research are just one way of conducting research; other existing models of research—which have a long and storied history of use and effectiveness—can be used to reframe equity work in ways that are scientifically rigorous and honor the scope and body of community stories.

We want to acknowledge that sometimes we can experience frustration and think that all of the talking and planning isn't "doing" anything and seems to make no clearly defined forward progress. It can be easy to feel lost in the process, and we offer our stories as an example of reframing this perspective and providing hope for other communities who are working to address inequities in a way that honors their unique stories, peoples, and experiences. We emphasize that coming together and holding space to listen to each other is not only extremely important, but necessary when addressing inequities and working together to build a more just and equitable future that aims to truly decolonize long-standing systems of oppression. The process of community collaboration is how we build trusting relationships, plan successful and sustainable projects, and celebrate each other's accomplishments—in other words, Indigenous research is much more than just results. Our equity work centers not on strategies for 1 to 3 years down the road, or even 30 years down the road, but "seven generations" into the future. We recognize that while we will not see the full realization of what this work aims to do, nor will we witness a complete transition to a just and equitable future in the Central Coast, what we can offer to future generations is a contribution to honoring Indigenous wisdom and values as we shift research frameworks to be actively decolonial and to serve communities more equitably in our collective struggle and aspirations for a truly sustainable, resilient, and justice-centered equitable future.

## End Notes

1. https://centralcoastequity.org/
2. https://centralcoastequity.org/regional-equity-study/

## References

Archibald, J. A. (2008). *Indigenous storywork: Educating the heart, mind, body, and spirit*. UBC Press.

Bryson, J. M., Crosby, B. C., & Middleton Stone, M. (2015). Designing and implementing cross-sector collaborations: Needed and challenging. *Public Administration Review* 75(5), 647–663.

Clauss-Ehlers, C. S., Chiriboga, D. A., Hunter, S., Roysircar, G., & Yammala-Nara, P. (2019). APA Multicultural guidelines executive summary: Ecological approach to context, identity, and intersectionality. *American Psychologist, 74*(2), 232–244.

Evolve Equity. (2023). *Strategic planning workgroup summary report*. Evolve Equity Psychology, Inc.

Fast, E., & Kovach, M. (2019). Community relationships within Indigenous methodologies. In S. Windchief & T. San Pedro (Eds.), *Applying Indigenous research methods: Storying with peoples and communities*. Routledge.

Hearst, M. O., & Dutton, L. L. (2021). The future deserves better—seeking health equity through interprofessional education, cultural humility, and understanding structural context. *Journal of Interprofessional Care, 35*, 1–2.

King, L., & Guillory, G. (2015). *GONA/GOAN curriculum & facilitation guide*. Substance Abuse and Mental Health Services Administration. https://www.samhsa.gov/sites/default/files/gona-goan-curriculum-facilitator-guide.pdf

Kuokkanen, R. (2007). *Reshaping the university: Responsibility, Indigenous epistemes, and the logic of the gift*. UCB Press.

Monchalin, L. (2016). *The colonial problem: An indigenous perspective on crime and injustice in Canada*. University of Toronto Press.

O'Connor, A., Pastor, M., & Vargas, M. (2021). *Towards a just and equitable Central Coast*. Central Coast Regional Equity Initiative. https://centralcoastequity.org/regional-equity-study/.

Sefa Dei, G. J. (2013). Critical perspectives of Indigenous research. *The Journal of Socialist Studies*, *9*, 27–38.

Shirley, V. J., & Angulo, D. (2019). Enacting Indigenous research methods: Centering Diné epistemology to guide the process. In S. Windchief & T. San Pedro (Eds.), *Applying Indigenous research methods: Storying with peoples and communities*. Routledge.

Tuck, E., & Yang. K. W. (2012). Decolonization is not a metaphor. *Decolonization: Indigeneity, Education & Society*, *1*(1), 1–40.

Wilson, S. (2008). *Research is ceremony: Indigenous research methods*. Fernwood.

Zavala, M. (2013). What do we mean by decolonizing research strategies? Lessons from decolonizing, Indigenous research projects in New Zealand and Latin America. *Decolonization: Indigeneity, Education, & Society*, *2*(1), 55–71.

**CHAPTER 8**

# Commitment to Pedagogical Partners in Early Childhood

*Paige Bray and Erin Kenney*

THIS CHAPTER IS an analysis of how early childhood practitioners acquire knowledge of equitable practices and work in context-specific communities to implement them. Beginning with setting a global aspirational policy, we explore who defines equitable practice in early childhood. Enactment of an aspirational policy on the national level is explicated, utilizing the United States early childhood workforce and National Association for the Education of Young Children as relevant examples. Finally, at the state and community level, insights and vignettes illustrate elements of how values-informed partnerships are contributing to the early childhood landscape. Implications for community-engaged scholarship and amplification of equitable practice in community settings relevant to early childhood families and practitioners are explicated. Throughout this chapter, we present a series of *authentic inquiry questions* designed to orient the reader in our reflective, critical thought process.

The care and attention given to early childhood education has traditionally been occupied by inequities and apathy in the United States. Given recent societally altering events, there is renewed attention to early childhood as a necessary component of workforce development. With the commodification of early care and education, culturally sustaining, developmentally appropriate learning opportunities are neglected in favor of one-size-fits-all educational practices. This standardization leads to a lack of equitable investment in humanity and our collective future. Given these phenomena, we critically inquire: *what does equitable practice look like at the global, national, state, and local community levels?*

## Setting Aspirational Policy—The Global Landscape

The space between birth and compulsory schooling has historically been occupied by inequities and indifference in the United States. In examining these inequities, *we critically inquire: given shared human experience forges and informs intersectional values, how does this confluence result in a shared aspirational policy?*

The landscape of early childhood in the United States has historically been a collection of conflicting assertions and at times differing values. For example, how does one balance the desire to nurture and educate young children with the rising cost of childcare (the average cost of care in the United States has risen 220% in the last three decades) and limits to family budgeted resources (Fillion, 2022)? How do government entities balance the burden to taxpayers with the consistently underfunded educational system (which often fails to include the early years as a time frame critical to human development)? Given the return on investment is thoroughly researched and documented, why does society fail to invest in our youngest community members (Heckman, 2023; Karoly et al., 2005)?

Despite these tensions in the United States, shared aspirational policy has been achieved on a global scale. The 1989 Convention on the Rights of the Child established an international shared set of intersectional values and principles (United Nations, 1989). Since its adoption by all member nations on November 20, 1989 in a General Assembly of the United Nations, 169 countries have ratified the convention. Solely absent is the United States. Despite their representatives' direct involvement in drafting the convention and adoption, the United States has failed to ratify the convention (Blanchfield, 2015).

The Convention on the Rights of the Child establishes inalienable rights for all children, giving agency to the youth of the world (Unicef, n.d.). Youth is broadly defined by this convention as children under the age of 18. Our focus on early childhood narrows this definition to children under the age of 8. Youth agency is the desire and ability of children to make decisions about their own lives including their local communities (International Youth Foundation, 2023). Agency for young children underpins critical developmental milestones that serve to assure optimal outcomes into adulthood. The development of a belief in themselves, their abilities, and an understanding of the abilities of others is key to establishing agency in young children. Through developmentally appropriate and culturally grounded authentic experiences, the child attains solutions-based competence and sense of self. Learning the skills associated with agency enables individuals to engage in community building and improvement as developmentally appropriate. The epistemological foundation for this argument is well established (Collins, 2000). In short, children who are supported in their abilities to take control of their actions and consequences become adults who possess the skills necessary to steward their life and navigate its complexities.

In light of the importance of establishing agency, the United States' failure to ratify the Convention on the Rights of the Child is particularly egregious. Who ensures these rights are granted to children in this country? Anyone engaged in the work of nurturing and educating young children has reason to invest in ensuring children possess those inalienable rights and agency aforementioned. These pedagogical partners include (but are not limited to): educators, caregivers, parents, early interventionists, social workers, mentors, health professionals, spiritual leaders, and peers. Pedagogical partnership therefore may take place in a variety of community-based settings and structures. These individuals become co-constructors of a child's care and educational pathway(s), enabling them to fulfill their optimal developmental trajectory(s). The intersection of these pedagogical partners (stakeholders) in their shared commitment to children's agency provides ample opportunity to engage in the work of raising children. Furthermore, compelling pedagogical partnerships promote practitioners' critical implementation of teaching practices that are culturally sustaining and developmentally appropriate.

## Enacting Aspirational Policy—The National Landscape

Since 2020, there is increased attention to the importance of early childhood care as fundamental to the functioning of our nation's workforce (Bassok et al., 2023; McLean et al., 2021; Thorpe et al., 2020; Zinsser et al., 2019). As the national landscape has and is changing, the development of the early childhood workforce becomes essential (Office of Early Childhood Development, 2023). In order for the capitalist machine to keep grinding, people must work to earn enough capital to take care of themselves, their family, their community, continuing in an endless cycle of labor and consumption. The role of early childhood care in this country is in part a necessary component of workforce development. Unlike other nations that provide months or years of multigenerational family leave options to support foundational relationships, we provide limited, underfunded options that remove material opportunities and family choices in parenting as well as create economic burden. By extension, considerations for the importance of family resources and their role in creating a sustainable daily routine for young children are ignored (Bernheimer et al., 1990; Weisner, 2002). With the commodification of early care and education, culturally sustaining, developmentally appropriate learning opportunities are neglected in favor of one-size-fits-all educational curriculum and practices.

Equitable practices that meet the needs of each child are informed by research and data; however, many start as theory (Antony, 2022; Bronfenbrenner, 1992; Bruner, 1984; Catherine et al., 2020; Cooks, 2010; Eun, 2019; Freire, 1985, 2018; Hausfather, 1996; hooks, 2014; Montessori, 1949/1988) or aspirational policies such as the Convention on the Rights of the Child (United Nations, 1989). These equitable practices enact aspirational policy in context-specific ways that meet the needs, for example, physical, intellectual, social, emotional, of each child. These practices are what are best for children. While these early experiences may also permit parents, grandparents, and other primary care takers to go to work, children having these early experiences across the birth to age 8 span in settings of their family's choice matters. These settings can include a variety of spaces such as at home, family care, community-based centers, and school-based settings. The family's right to choose an appropriate early childhood setting is a key indicator of honoring caregiver knowledge of what is best for the child.

The early childhood workforce, as in the adults who care for and educate children from birth to age 8, are essential to the larger national economic "productivity," yet they are also the perpetual disruptors and reimaginers of early care and educational practices. In the United States, where the government writ large resists committing to global, human understanding of basic child rights, we ask: *Who defines what is equitable practice and how might it lead to the fulfillment of an aspirational policy?* In the absence of steadfast advocacy and responsiveness at governmental levels, we in the United States have child advocacy movements of concerned community members and dedicated organizations, such as the National Association for the Education of Young Children (NAEYC), as dependable advocates. The National Association for the Education of Young Children's professional standards and competencies for early childhood educators continue an enduring commitment to equity in early care and education. As is imperative for the changing landscape of early childhood these standards evolve and are updated to reflect changes in research and understandings of developmentally appropriate practice. Implementation of these standards is the responsibility of preparation and practice institutions. Power to the profession is a national collaboration that has "established a unifying framework of recommendations on educator roles and responsibilities, aligned preparation pathway(s), profession compensation and a supportive infrastructure with shared accountability" (NAEYC, 2023).

In considering the complete early childhood workforce trifecta, a) the need for early care and education so adults be active contributors in the national workforce; b) the impact of early childhood care and education professionals doing their work as essential labor in the national workforce; and c) the equity advocates who perpetuate, disrupt, and reimagine early care and educational practices for the next generation, we ask: *What do equitable practices among the early childhood workforce that both support young children's agency and meet context-specific community needs look like?* As we have addressed the multi-faceted workforce issue, we continue by exploring what context-specific means across generations and locations.

While we problematize the assumption that institutionalized preschool education meets the needs of the whole child, this snapshot from the National Center for Educational Statistics captures enrollment in early schooling and the distinctly different state-based experience (see Figure 8.1). This map does not capture the disparity of access to quality care within and across states for those families that would want it. Neither does the map reflect those who do not elect to enroll their young child earlier in an educational system that has historically underserved, marginalized or undermined them (Ainscow, 2020; Children's Defense Fund, 2021; Connecticut State Department of Education, n.d.; Gaias et al., 2022; Iruka et al., 2023; Learning Policy Institute; 2021).

At first look this map captures the percentage of 3- to 5-year-olds enrolled in school by state. A more detailed review informs us of where there are the least number of children engaged in early education. We know that early experiences

**Figure 8.1:**
*Percentage of 3- to 5-year-olds enrolled in school, by state and comparison with the national average; 2019*

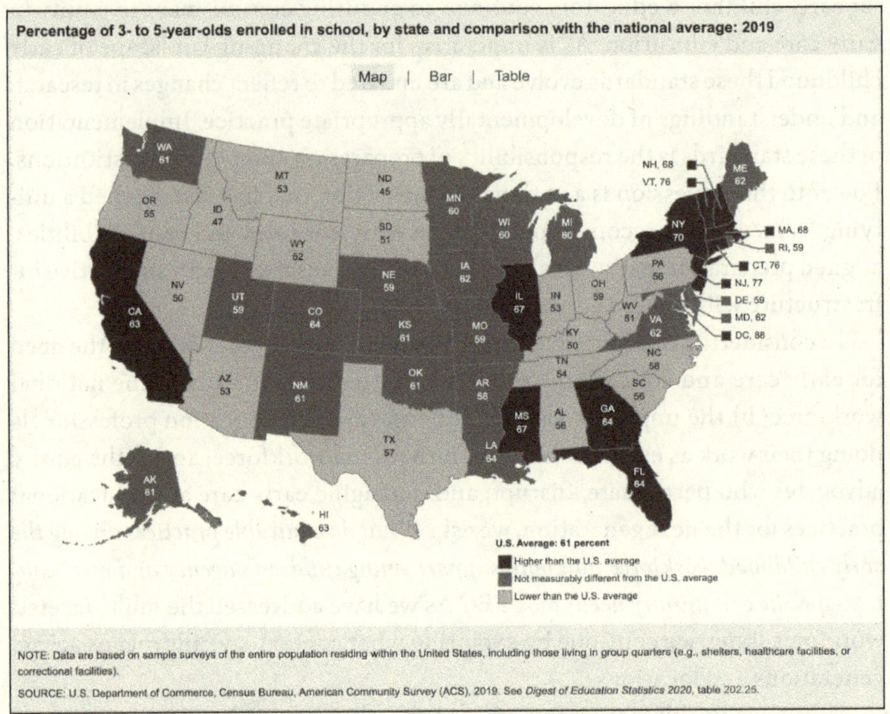


support human development (Hardy et al., 2021; Heckman et al., 2010; Mapping Childhood Opportunity, 2021; Urahn, 2009), yet the standardization and institutionalizing of experience lead to a lack of equitable investment in humanity and our collective future (Iruka et al., 2023; Jones et al., 2020; Lillard et al., 2017; Nation's Report Card, 2022).

Before compulsory or early schooling begins, there is a critical 3-year window of infant and toddler development (Bates et al., 2021; Borchers et al., 2021; Edvoll et al., 2023; Smith-Flores & Feigenson, 2022; Wallace & Manz, 2023). The full early childhood span continues beyond these initial years up to the age of 8 and requires integrated nurturing of the whole child for healthy development and overall wellness. The U.S. policies neither support every child's access to basic needs nor provide the family unit the mechanisms to support their child. These mechanisms include access to paid family leave, affordable food, and housing.

The one area that has seen positive gains for those in the first 8 years of life is the number of children in the United States with health insurance (see Figure 8.2). While this does not guarantee better quality of care, preventive care, or quality of life, the access is a step towards supporting the healthy development of young children. This investment in young children is not devoid of systemic and implicit bias that impacts the care received (Hammond, 2014, 2021). This commitment to care is not seen for the adults and family members as

**Figure 8.2:**
*Health Insurance Coverage Status and Type of Coverage for Children Under 19: 2020 and 2021*

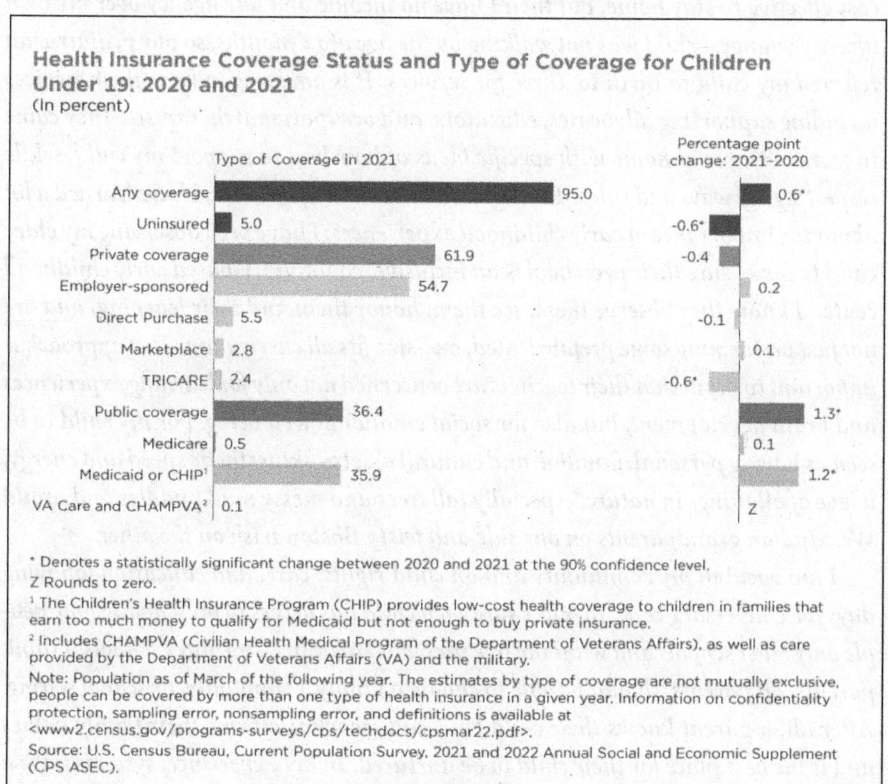

evidenced by the statistically significant increase in the 2021 maternal mortality rates (Hoyert, 2022). What increased rates of insured children does is increase wellness checks and early developmental milestone checks so that health care can provide early investments and interventions towards whole child wellness.

What follows is a vignette demonstrating the complexity of the early childhood landscape for parents and providers. In short, this is one composite example of what raising young children can look like in the United States.

## Embodiment of the Layers of Early Childhood: A Vignette

*I am the parent of two young children, ages 2 and 4; the cost of full day care is over $1000 per month per child. It is not sustainable to try to pay this much, it is more cost effective to stay home, but then I have no income and lose agency over my own life. My youngest child was not walking by the age of 14 months, so our pediatrician referred my child to Birth to Three for services. It is amazing to have their services including supporting advocates, educators, and occupational therapists. They come to work with me at home with specific ideas of how best to support my child, while respecting my ways and rules. Through these positive experiences, I have learned a lot about the importance of early childhood experiences. I have been observing my elder child to make sure their preschool is an inclusive, community-based early childhood center. I know they observe them, see them, honor them and their learning, and are not just performing some prefabricated, one-size fits all curriculum. This approach is important to me in that their teachers are concerned not only for learning experiences and brain development, but also for social emotional well being. For my child to be seen as having personal, familial, and cultural assets—kinesthetic speed and energy, a love of all things in nature, especially tall trees and messy mud puddles and proud West Indian grandparents on one side and feisty Boston Irish on the other.*

*I am vocal in my community and on child rights, care, and education lobbying days for Universal Pre-K, to make sure each child has access to preschool. Some people only trust schools and want the free preschool to be in elementary schools. I think parents, all parents, should be able to choose a family, community, or school setting. After all, a parent knows their child best, can see what affirms their family values and is the best place for their child to be nurtured. In my experience, systems have a long history of tearing some of us down and bombarding others with negative messages for being any and all kinds of "different" but that is just systemic oppression. Fear-based thinking that lacks curiosity. Social pressure and shaming keep children, really all of us, from learning from our mistakes. After all, mistakes are just feedback or data telling you to try something different or letting you know that option did not work. Only through repeated negative responses to a miss or an error do children get wired (literally in their brain and nervous system) to have an emotional response to mistakes. Ironically, the emotional response only shuts down the thinking brain, limits the ability to reason, or even "perform" well. So why would I want to send my children to a place that does not like, honor, and lift them up? If people are not curious or inclusive and invested in building relationships, then I am not interested in my children spending time with them, even if it is free school.*

*I know from the annual early childhood conversations conference that all the faculty from the early childhood community colleges and the undergraduate and graduate colleges and universities come together to advocate for children rights. This conference, which began as a multi-community workshop that amplified parent knowledge, has grown over two decades into a state-wide, collaborative event honoring the work of both providers and families. The conference brings parents, providers, and community together to support meaningful early childhood experiences. I hear these advocates discuss the need to increase the pay of teachers and I wonder, "How can I have to pay so much and still the actual teachers are being paid so little?!" Many of us want to grow in our lives, in our daily work, and I see how working together can bring more learning and professional opportunities. It reminds me of last week at the Dismantling Systemic Racism Conference, when I saw how equity is a commitment for those truly doing their own work so they can embrace all children. Lifted up by a state, regional education center with a core mission of racial justice, this conference draws upon the authentic successes and challenges occurring across the state as experienced by communities, schools, before and after care providers, educator preparation, and community change efforts. There are fancy Blue Ribbon Panels and other forums, but they don't always reflect all that I value for my children. What I value most is humans, as individuals and in collectives, who are the ones that enact changes and build capacity.*

## Conducing Aspirational Policy—The Local Landscape

In this section we offer a critical examination of how people consume and produce knowledge of equitable practices in just ways using context-specific networks as the locus of exchange. We, the authors, come to this work with a 13-year collaboration and commitment to community-engaged research. Paige is a daughter from the western Rockies and mother of Jewish sons. As a queer white, cis female in mid-life she has spent a lifetime engaging in women-center justice fights continuously redefined by the intersection of race, class, religion, and releasing of binary thinking. An advocate for children, she has had many jobs in both community-based and higher education settings. Erin is a daughter from the hills of Connecticut and proud aunt to many niblings. As a white, cis female she has spent her time engaging at the intersection of early childhood education and developmental psychology. She is steeped in the commitment to bridge the gap between the two fields by utilizing participatory, action research methodology to engage marginalized voices in change work.

With these distinct and shared perspectives, we critically inquire: *in what ways do resource allocations amplify networks and support justice work?* We illuminate five examples that build out from individual action to full-scale systemic work. While justice work is never that linear, this amalgamated case seeks to capture the notion, "Justice is what love looks like in public" (West, 2017). Each pedagogical partnership here builds up or draws upon a network that shares justice commitments in the early childhood space. A common thread through these examples is that in our current capitalist, representative democracy, the resource of human capital, including paid and invisible labor, is paired with fiscal resources to leverage desired impact at some targetable level. Despite early childhood being framed as women's work, undervalued and thus misunderstood as simple or lacking complexity and research-driven practices, opportunities such as the ones in this section defy this expectation. They center hard-won clarity of shared commitments to community and amplify that change can happen and has over time, around the world, generation after generation. What follows shares how in the contemporary landscape networking of resources has served to further justice for young children.

An early childhood educator in a community care setting makes half, or less than half, that of an early childhood educator in government-funded early intervention programs or public school settings (See Appendix E, Taskforce on Early Childhood Workforce Development, 2023). Each person could be doing the same or similar foundational developmental work with the children, and their families as partners, during the first 8 years of life. In 2023, the hourly rate of pay, even in resourced states, is higher at big box stores or fast food chain restaurants than for early care and education workers outside of the public system. This means those in community settings cannot pay for their own basic needs, including affording the cost of care for their own children while they work.

Community, state, and national organizations have been increasingly active since the 2020 pandemic reality of a lack of available childcare (among other factors) kept parents home and out of the workforce. The values-grounded work of these childhood advocates is imperative as families and communities seek to increase options for meaningful early childhood experiences. One example of new intersecting efforts to include a variety of stakeholders is the AMI-USA Human Rights and Social Justice advisory committee (more at: https://amiusa.org/about/equity-and-inclusion/). This committee connects with local Montessori representatives of the Montessori Public Policy Initiative (more at: https://montessoriadvocacy.org/connect/find-a-state-group/) to amplify valuable, credentialed early childhood care and Montessori early education happening, birth through age 8, that is not recognized by care-rating, accreditation, and credit-bearing systems. Another example is BIPOC-owned urban community early care and education centers that have formed a network, a linked set of centers, to leverage not only operational but legislative power. These multi-level networking efforts from local to state to national audiences not only serve as catalysts for change, but also provide generative exchanges that sustain hope, professional growth, and expressions of personal commitments.

While our work in a decade-long, university and statewide parent co-researcher partnership is extensively explicated in other spaces (more at: https://parentii.wordpress.com/), the work was a significant strand in the knowledge development work and system changing efforts that transformed the landscape of early childhood in the American state of Connecticut. Regional philanthropy in "learning agreements" with a national foundation pivoted to inclusive knowledge development (Frusciante, 2014). This change reframed the proposal-funding-outcomes sequence of grant making to an equity-driven and capacity building investment(s) in people and community.

Specifically, parent learning and leadership engagement occurred through collaborative action inquiry across the state's four major urban centers along with the largest micropolitan areas in the United States. In this early work (Bray et al., 2014), action inquiry was brought to parent leaders as a tool that they honed for their own use and change agendas. The outgrowth of this phase of the work was a parent-constructed community conversations guide in English and Spanish (Bray et al., 2013).

With a commitment to dissemination of public scholarship, our ongoing, multi-directional, capacity-building endeavor consciously placed parents at the center of a parent education work (Bray & Kenney, 2014). We then extended the project from inquiry to more overtly participatory action research work with parents seeing themselves as co-researchers who possess valued knowledge. Amplifying the voices of parents occurred through accessible dissemination and in formats the parents could leverage directly (See Parentii YouTube channel: https://youtu.be/25GEqHrPWYY). By parents claiming the opportunity to build their capacity, we observed improved outcomes in their own lives as well as in the lives of the children they nurtured.

Ultimately, this multi-year, community-building "Discovery Network" effort, that included our parent leadership work (Bray & Kenney, 2015), established our current Office of Early Childhood with a governor's cabinet level commissioner. By pairing the roles-inclusive early childhood collaborative cabinet as a structural model for decision-making, with extensive discovery communities having established integrated resources and infrastructure, the structural creation of the Office of Early Childhood was made possible and systemic change brought forth.

Once established as a state government agency, Connecticut's Office of Early Childhood became subject to distinct political optics. While being integrated into the state government system provides legitimacy it comes with many limitations, including a public alignment with the elected state leadership. The access to shared work, among and across related agencies, for change that serves the children of a state or municipality is an aspect of the "power to the profession" (NAEYC, 2023) again, hard won at the national level. Yet, there is power from the margins, the unbridled ability to call out injustice, unacceptable practices, and oppressive policy and see the possibility of change from outside of the existing mechanisms and capitalist machine. In a resistance to binary thinking, people have leveraged this work to support radical, systemic change. This leveraging includes data-informed, research-driven decision-making that serves to intentionally amplify the voices of the marginalized-children, and in this example women, queer, and nonbinary parents. The input of these marginalized groups and the knowledge they produce is valued as the wisdom that comes from lived experience.

After the formation of the agency, a state-wide Office of Early Childhood initiative implemented funding NAEYC accreditation opportunities for all 2 and 4 year higher education early childhood educator preparation institutions. This one effort has spurred systems change that requires discourse about quality care, impactful educational experiences, and provides pathways for early care and educators to have a career arc that includes significant increases in pay. Perhaps most importantly, this alignment of educational opportunities provides a high school to bachelor's degree pathway that decenters a residential undergraduate experience and is inclusive of students who live at home, maintain jobs, have young children, and other responsibilities. Part of this systemic change has created co-construction of program design along with intentionally curated content (more at: https://ectacenter.org/about/osep-ec-centers.asp) that incorporates culturally informed early intervention practices (more at: https://www.dec-sped.org/ei-ecse-standards) that propel the work, the field, and the profession forward.

Philanthropic organizations have had an enduring influence on early childhood from child labor laws to employer-sponsored early care and education. Untethered by politics or legislation, philanthropy-supported systemic work continues to be a formidable force in early childhood in the United States. In the global Montessori education space, multiyear, multimillion dollar competitive grants and philanthropic giving have created spaces for critical examination of deficit-behavior schooling, narrow instruction that meets the needs of a small subset of learners. The work around the globe, connected through continuation of Montessori's work in human development and education, has challenged the underestimation of human capacity. Some boundaryless efforts include the Montessori Community Glossary Project furthering a contemporary and relevant understanding of Montessori through "an open source glossary project created by and for the Montessori community." The Montessori Glossary is an evolving, iterative, co-construction project grounded in shared knowledge and authority" (more at: www.montessoriglossary.org).

More geographically specific efforts include increasing access to undergraduate education through pedagogical partnership programing and proportional award scholarships that support matriculation to graduation. Intentionally, student experience–centered scholarship awards are offered as a percentage of total tuition cost by term so the actual award dollars keep pace with the actual cost across all 4 years (University of Hartford, 2017). Historically, attrition from institutions of higher education has included those students who cannot fill the gap between fixed scholarship award dollars and even relatively small increases in tuition costs each year. Seeing a greater number of students have financial status changes during the COVID pandemic accentuated the fact that overdue tuition and compounding fees quickly become overwhelming for many students, many institutions of higher education waived fees (Purifoy et al., 2021). In the context of low-cost or even free community college settings, even the smallest fees can bring a halt to a student's educational progress (Butrymowicz et al., 2022). Specific community innovations like this make visible opportunities for other more equity-driven policies such as income-driven loan repayments (Federal Student Aid, n.d.) a small effort in the compounded, unjust financial legacy of our country. Implications of the networking and justice work in early childhood and community-engaged scholarship will now be explored.

## Implications: Community-Engaged Scholarship in Early Childhood Contexts

When the result of pedagogical partnership is an aspirational policy, we inquire who is included in the conversations that inform said policy. Furthermore, by what criteria are individuals allowed to participate in the conversation(s) and what value is given to the voices of those included, marginalized, and excluded. An aspirational policy that will stand the test of time requires representation of diverse viewpoints inclusive of marginalized voices whose message is valued and acted upon. There is an inherent value in being welcome to participate in these conversations and power in participation to shape future outcomes. Historically there exists a distinct lack of attention to the power structures and inequities that inform who is welcome to participate. To be truly intersectional in the approach to aspirational policy, we must ensure opportunities for those voices to be heard are not only available, but filled by carefully curated representatives of the population. In community-engaged sustainable practice, this means meeting individuals where they are and in the ways that they can contribute.

Equitable practice in community settings is often supported by community-engaged research funded by philanthropic and academic institutions. The values of these organizations may align or contrast with those intrinsic to equitable practice in community engagement. The structures inherent to these institutions and funded research, including such accepted practices as funding applications, grant reports, and Institutional Review Board review, may present barriers to meeting community members where they are and in the ways that they can contribute. Additionally, the institutional support structures may serve to hinder the momentum of community-engaged scholarship particularly when existing structures are narrow in scope.

Community-engaged scholars require radically different resources and approaches than what is allocated in the traditional research model. Engagement in communities requires investment in resources including: space to meet, time for engagement outside normal working hours, childcare, and access to academic materials both physical and virtual (Bray & Kenney, 2014). The willingness of institutions to accept the changing needs of community-engaged research and fund these vital resources varies and by extension informs what knowledge is produced. Additionally, community members may serve to further the work or hinder it. Individual community members and stakeholders may serve to assist community-engaged researchers in hearing all voices of the community or inhibit access in some way. The challenge of equitable community scholarship is finding the individuals who will champion the research and the means to work with those who would impede others in participating.

Community-engaged scholarship works to include local participants and stakeholders in shared goals for research. Effective community-engaged scholarship is grounded in a shared set of values and assumptions that allow for all voices including those typically excluded or marginalized to be heard. These assumptions include the research process as: a) engaged "with" people in a process, not "for" or "on" research subjects; b) a democratic, inclusive process that enables participation of all parent leaders while developing critical consciousness; c) an equitable process recognizing human capacity and an individual's ability to contribute; and d) a liberating and life-enhancing activity with the expressed commitment to practical outcomes that transform structures and relationships (Bray & Kenney, 2014, 2015; Bray et al., 2014).

Pedagogical partnerships in early childhood have the ability to be transformative for children and families at multiple targetable levels. Transformative social advocacy views children and their caregivers as catalysts for change, key to implementing the fundamental innovations explicated in this chapter. Work with, not on, community members that is designed to value shared goals and outcomes is the essence of equitable, community-engaged research practice. In keeping with the ponderings throughout this chapter we leave you with one last inquiry: *what equity-seeking, justice-driven changes are needed to ensure future generations can enact sustainable care and educational practices for children at global, national, state, and community levels?*

## References

Ainscow, M. (2020). Promoting inclusion and equity in education: Lessons from international experiences. *Nordic Journal of Studies in Educational Policy, (6)*1, 7–16.

Antony, E. M. (2022). Framing childhood resilience through Bronfenbrenner's ecological systems theory: A literature review. *Cambridge Educational Research E-journal, 9*, 244–257.

Bassok, D., Bellows, L., Markowitz, A. J., & Miller-Bains, K. (2023, April 11). *Building a professional early childhood workforce requires a "compensation-first" approach.* The Brookings Institution. https://www.brookings.edu/blog/brown-center-chalkboard/2023/04/11/building-a-professional-early-childhood-workforce-requires-a-compensation-first-approach/

Bates, R. A., Singletary, B., Dynia, J. M., & Justice, L. M. (2021). Temperament and sleep behaviors in infants and toddlers living in low-income homes. *Infant Behavior and Development, (65).*

Bernheimer, L. P., Gallimore, R., & Weisner, T. S. (1990). Ecocultural theory as a context for the individual family service plan. *Journal of Early Intervention, (14)*3.

Blanchfield, L. (2015). *The United Nations convention on the rights of the child.* Congressional Research Service. R40484. https://crsreports.congress.gov/

Borchers, L. R., Dennis, E. L., King, L. S., Humphreys, K. L., & Gotlib, I. H. (2021). Prenatal and postnatal depressive symptoms, infant white matter, and toddler behavioral problems. *Journal of Affective Disorders, (282)*, 465–471. https://doi.org/10.1016/j.jad.2020.12.075

Bronfenbrenner, U. (1992). *Ecological systems theory*. Jessica Kingsley Publishers.

Bray, P. M., Abubakar, D., Carter, W., Hernandez, C., Jackson, M., James, C., Kenney, E. M., Maciel-Andrews, Y., Peters, T., Petersen, C., & Woodworth, K. (2013). *Looking for answers together: How should we nurture children to be healthy and make better choices?* Kettering Foundation Issue Guide, invited manuscript. Connecticut dissemination by William Caspar Graustein Memorial Fund; National dissemination by National Issues Forum. https://parentii.files.wordpress.com/2019/12/looking-for-answers_graustein.pdf & https://parentii.files.wordpress.com/2019/12/graustein_span_mod_guide-3-11-14.pdf

Bray, P. M., & Kenney, E. M. (2014). Parent leaders taking the lead: Capacity building and co-constructed relevance in community-engaged research. *Journal of Public Scholarship in Higher Education, 4*, 93–109.

Bray, P. M., & Kenney, E. M. (2015). Parents as producers of enduring knowledge through inquiry. In *Disrupting Early Childhood Education Research* (pp. 57–70). Routledge.

Bray, P. M., Pedro, J., Kenney, E. M., & Gannotti, M. (2014). Collaborative action inquiry: A tool for, and result of, parent learning and leadership. *Journal of Community Engagement and Scholarship, 7*(1), 3–14.

Bruner, J. (1984). Vygotsky's zone of proximal development: The hidden agenda. *New Directions for Child Development, 23*, 93–97.

Butrymowicz, S., D'Amato, P. D., Kolodner, M., & Shalby, C. (2022, March 17). Overdue tuition and fees, even $41, can derail a community college education. *Los Angeles Times*. https://www.latimes.com/california/story/2022-03-17/overdue-tuition-and-fees-can-derail-community-college-education

Catherine, L. E., Javier, B., & Francisco, G. (2020). Four pillars of the Montessori method and their support by current neuroscience. *Mind, Brain, and Education, 14*(4), 322–334.

Children's Defense Fund. (2021). *The state of America's children 2021*. https://www.childrensdefense.org/state-of-americas-children/

Collins, P. H. (2000). *Black feminist thought: Knowledge, consciousness, and the politics of empowerment*. Routledge.

Connecticut State Department of Education. (n.d.). *Early childhood special education*. Connecticut's Official State Website. https://portal.ct.gov/SDE/Special-Education/Early-Childhood-Special-Education

Cooks, L. (2010). The (critical) pedagogy of communication and the (critical) communication of pedagogy. In D. L. Fassett & J. T. Warren (Eds.), *The SAGE handbook of communication and instruction*. SAGE Publications.

Edvoll, M., Kehoe, C. E., Trøan, A. S., Harlem, T. S., & Havighurst, S. S. (2023). The relations between parent and toddler emotional regulation. *Mental Health & Prevention, (30)*. https://doi.org/10.1016/j.mhp.2023.200266

Eun, B. (2019).The zone of proximal development as an overarching concept: A framework for synthesizing Vygotsky's theories. *Educational Philosophy and Theory, 51*(1), 18–30.

Federal Student Aid. (n.d.). *If your federal student loan payments are high compared to your income, you may want to repay your loans under an income-driven repayment plan*. U.S. Department of education. https://studentaid.gov/manage-loans/repayment/plans/income-driven

Fillion, J. (2022). Child care prices rose significantly in 2020: Continuing decades-long trend of major annual increases. *First Five Years Fund*. https://www.ffyf.org/child-care-prices-rose-significantly-in-2020-continuing-decades-long-trend-of-major-annual-increases/

Freire, P. (1985). *The politics of education: Culture, power, and liberation*. Greenwood Publishing Group.

Freire, P. (2018). *Pedagogy of the oppressed*. Bloomsbury Publishing USA.

Frusciante, A. (2014). Shifting from 'evaluation' to valuing: A six-year example of philanthropic practice change and knowledge development. *The Foundation Review, 6*(2), 10.

Gaias, L. M., Gal-Szabo, D. E., Shivers, E. M., & Kiche, S. (2022). From laissez-faire to anti-discrimination: How are race/ethnicity, culture, and bias integrated into multiple domains of practice in early childhood education? *Journal of Research in Childhood Education, 36*(2), 272–295.

Hammond, Z. (2014). *Culturally responsive teaching and the brain: Promoting authentic engagement and rigor among culturally and linguistically diverse students*. Corwin Press.

Hammond, Z. (2021). Liberatory education: Integrating the science of learning and culturally responsive practice. *American Educator, 45*(2), 4.

Hardy, E., Joshi, P., Leonardos, M., & Acevedo-Garcia, D. (2021). *Advancing racial equity through neighborhood informed early childhood policies*. Diversity data kids. https://www.diversitydatakids.org/research-library/research-report/advancing-racial-equity-through-neighborhood-informed-early?utm_source=email&utm_medium=email&utm_campaign=A4ES

Hausfather, S. J. (1996). Vygotsky and schooling: Creating a social context for learning. *Action in Teacher Education, 18*(2), 1–10.

Heckman, J. J. (2023). *Early investments and return on investment for ECE/childcare*. The Heckman Equation. https://heckmanequation.org

Heckman, J. J, Moon, S. H., Pinto, R., Savelyey, P. A., & Yavitz, A. (2010). The rate of return to the High/Scope Perry preschool program. *Journal of Public Economics, 94*(1–2), 114–128. https://doi.org/10.1016/j.jpubeco.2009.11.001

hooks, b. (2014). *Teaching to transgress*. Routledge.

Hoyert, D. L. (2022). *Maternal mortality rates in the United States, 2021*. NCHS health e-stats. https://doi.org/10.15620/cdc:113967

International Youth Foundation. (2023, April 29). *What is youth agency?* International Youth Foundation. https://iyfglobal.org/youth-agency

Iruka, I. U., Blanchard, S., Commons, C. M., Guzman, R., Kasprzak, C. M., Kemp, P., Newton, J., Perry, S., Study, W., Talley, M., Flores, C. T., Turner, T., & Williams, C. A. (2023). *Fact sheet: Advancing racial equity in early intervention and preschool special education.* Early childhood technical assistance center. https://ectacenter.org/topics/racialequity/factsheet-racialequity-2023.asp

Jones, T. M., Fleming, C., Williford, A., & Research and Evaluation Team of Seattle Public Schools. (2020). Racial equity in academic success: The role of school climate and social emotional learning. *Children and Youth Services Review, 119*. https://doi.org/10.1016/j.childyouth.2020.105623

Karoly, L. A., Kilburn, M. R., & Cannon, J. (2005). *Early childhood interventions: Proven results, future promise.* The Rand Corporation. https://www.rand.org/content/dam/rand/pubs/monographs/2005/RAND_MG341.pdf

Learning Policy Institute. (2021). *Building a national early childhood education system that works.* https://learningpolicyinstitute.org/product/early-childhood-education-system-2021-brief?gclid=CjwKCAjwjMiiBhA4EiwAZe6jQ5jnok9ABf3IpylYjFrnnvasW6qH5Fbw6IZhSd68oU6CyTu_i7wzmhoCYg4QAvD_BwE

Lillard, A. S., Heise, M. J., Richey, E. M., Tong, X., Hart, A., & Bray, P. M. (2017). Montessori preschool elevates and equalizes child outcomes: A longitudinal study. *Frontiers in Psychology, (8)*, 17–83.

Mapping Child Opportunity. (2021). Alliance for early success. https://www.diversitydatakids.org/maps/?utm_source=email&utm_medium=email&utm_campaign=A4ES

McLean, C., Austin, L. J., Whitebook, M., & Olson, K. L. (2021). *Early childhood workforce index 2020.* Center for the study of child care employment. University of California, Berkeley.

Montessori, M. (1949/1988). *The absorbent mind.* Clio Press.

National Association for the Education of Young Children (NAEYC). (2023) Professional Standards and Competencies for Early Childhood Educators. Retrieved from: https://www.naeyc.org/resources/position-statements/professional-standards-competencies

Nation's Report Card, The. (2022). https://nces.ed.gov/nationsreportcard/

Office of Early Childhood Development. (2023). *Resources to support early care and education workforce strategies.* Office of Administration for Children and Families. https://www.acf.hhs.gov/ecd/initiatives/strategy-resources-address-early-care-and-education-ece-workforce-shortage

Purifoy, P., Avi-Yonah, S., & Bloomberg. (2021). Colleges tap into stimulus funds to wipe unpaid fees for low-income students. *Fortune.* https://fortune.com/2021/08/01/colleges-universities-pandemic-stimulus-funds-wipe-out-fees-low-income-students/

Smith-Flores, A. S., & Feigenson, L. (2022). 'Yay! Yuck!' toddlers use others' emotional responses to reason about hidden objects. *Journal of Experimental Child Psychology, (221).* https://doi.org/10.1016/j.jecp.2022.105464

Taskforce on Early Childhood Workforce Development. (2023). *Early childhood workforce final report.* Connecticut General Assembly. https://www.cga.ct.gov/ed/taskforce.asp?TF=20220919_Taskforce%20on%20Early%20Childhood%20Workforce%20Development

Thorpe, K., Jansen, E., Sullivan, V., Irvine, S., McDonald, P., & Early Years Workforce Study Team. (2020). Identifying predictors of retention and professional wellbeing of the early childhood education workforce in a time of change. *Journal of Educational Change, 21,* 623–647.

Unicef. (n.d.). *Convention on the rights of the child: The children's version.* https://www.unicef.org/child-rights-convention/convention-text-childrens-version\

United Nations. (1989). Convention on the rights of the child. United Nations. https://www.ohchr.org/en/instruments-mechanisms/instruments/convention-rights-child

University of Hartford. (2017, June 22). Walton Family Foundation awards $4.8 million dollar grant to the University of Hartford and the Montessori Training Center Northeast to create Montessori Bachelor's degree program [press release]. https://www.hartford.edu/news/press-releases/2017/06/montessori_program.aspx

Urahn, S. K. (2009). *Fund early childhood education.* The PEW Charitable Trusts. https://www.pewtrusts.org/en/about/news-room/opinion/2009/10/07/fund-early-childhood-education

Wallace, L. E., & Manz, P. H. (2023). Addressing the needs of infants and toddlers exposed to maltreatment: Examining the impact of an integrated early head start & children youth services program. *Children and Youth Services Review, (146).* https://doi.org/10.1016/j.childyouth.2023.106808

Weisner, T. S. (2002). Ecocultural understanding of children's developmental pathways. *Human Development, 45*(4), 275–281. https://doi.org/10.1159/000064989

West, C. (2017, October 4). Tenderness in education: Harvard Graduate School of Education ASKWITH forum lecture series.

Zinsser, K. M., Main, C., Torres, L., & Connor, K. (2019). Patching the pathway and widening the pipeline: Models for developing a diverse early childhood workforce in Chicago. *American Journal of Community Psychology, 63*(3–4), 459–471.

**CHAPTER 9**

# Embracing the Journey: Growing Educational Pathways for Food Sovereignty

*Adrienne Cachelin, Leah Joyner, Paul Kuttner, Gilberto Rejon Magana, Elizabeth Montoya, Jarred Martinez, Keri Taddie, Blanca Yagüe, and Debolina Banerjee*

*"I didn't spend 8 days crossing that damn desert to give up."*

— SLC parent and partner

## Introduction

IN MARCH OF 2020, the global shutdown quieted the streets of Salt Lake City (SLC). Many residents hunkered down, gathering what food and supplies they could to brace for this new reality. For over 23,000 students living on the city's Westside, the situation jeopardized access not only to education but also to school food programs. These students already experienced heightened food insecurity and educational inequity, living in neighborhoods shaped by histories of food apartheid and educational disinvestment (Joyner, Yagüe, et al., 2022; Wood, 2015). And yet, somehow, these unprecedented times also ignited dreams of a more equitable world where all bodies and minds would be nourished.

As community-based researchers working on food justice and educational equity, the intertwined political economic roots of these issues were already clear. In this moment, these issues became visceral and called for informed action. Through the course of our research, we listened to urban farmers who dreamt of a post-COVID landscape in which local, ecologically sound food systems embedded in a diversity of land use strategies and relations would create a peoples' food sovereignty. We listened to food access advocates who envisaged a food system in which families have the right to access culturally sustaining, nutritious foods, based not in emergency funding but in a more equitable system overall. We listened to Westside residents who envisioned food as a right that is not reliant on an already marginalizing school system. And we listened to school district partners, students, community education advocates, and parents on the Westside who, recognizing the diminished sense of belonging resulting from busing their students to distant high schools, dreamt of a community high school that builds pathways to higher education.

Together we—a collective of resident leaders, organizers, educators, and researchers—launched a project to simultaneously promote food sovereignty and educational justice through urban agricultural initiatives. At the *core* of this project is the idea that culturally sustaining urban agriculture, when connected to schools and universities, can increase the ability of marginalized students to assert their right to belong in school in the short term, and foster local autonomous food production in the long term. At the *heart* of this chapter is the magic of our journey, listening and critically reflecting on our assumptions, leading us to embrace a community–university praxis that is ongoing and iterative.

## Who we are

Our group of authors includes university and public-school faculty and staff, leaders of nonprofit groups and community residents. Many of us have worked together for more than 10 years on a variety of environmental justice related projects. We also work with student researchers under the auspices of the SPARC Environmental Justice Lab (SPARC), a group committed to enacting principles of critical participatory action research to understand social and environmental health disparities and co-create strategies to achieve justice. SPARC is an acronym for three intertwined pillars of our work including:

- Student Pathways are central to our research process. Student lab members are learning, developing, and critically engaging in ways that promote ongoing reflection, empowerment, and social change. The term "pathways" reflects our long-term commitment to a thematic area over several student cohorts. Student pathways begin with critical participatory research that may lead to theses, dissertations, or paid positions that produce academic and community-facing outputs.

- Action Research is a key element to all projects, as is the generation of knowledge. Our research is designed *by* and *with* those taking action towards environmental justice. Our research outcomes are designed to be accessible and available to inform policy and change-making at multiple scales, from community initiatives to nonprofit programs, mutual aid projects, and municipal bodies such as city councils, school boards, and state legislatures.
- Critical community engagement manifests in SPARC projects as we aim to avoid the ahistorical and nonpolitical approaches that have traditionally characterized social science and ecological research. SPARC projects engage a paradigm that sees research as a product of both community expertise and interdisciplinary academic training. Community members, who have historically been disempowered by extractive research processes, are co-researchers and direct beneficiaries of the products and processes of engaged research.

In this work, our group of co-researchers/authors came to better understand the local political and economic factors responsible for geographies of inequity and their impacts on food and educational justice. Subsequently, integrating distinct lines of research while critically reflecting on our findings and assumptions has allowed for the creation of a promising new program.

Our work is driven by critical geographic theory that examines relationships between space, place, groups, and power (Reynolds et al., 2020) where the connection between theory and practice, that is, praxis can reveal and transform unjust power dynamics (Savin-Baden & Major, 2013). Ultimately, as "stakeholders and action researchers [we] co-create knowledge that is pragmatically useful and grounded in local knowledge" (Denzin & Lincoln, 2018). In the next section, we describe the socio-political context regarding food apartheid and educational equity before describing the ways that our praxis evolved resulting in a collaborative program.

## Geographies of Inequity in Salt Lake City

### *Context*

The COVID-19 pandemic revealed a host of preexisting racial and socio-economic inequities across the United States and exposed their intersecting roots. A particularly insidious convergence of these inequities emerged when the closing of schools jeopardized free and reduced food programs on which many Westside families depend. Salt Lake City's Westside is home to much of the city's immigrant and refugee community, including 75% of Salt Lake's Latinx population (University Neighborhood Partners, 2019). The Westside is a vibrant community, where residents report a sense of pride in the abundant green spaces, parks, trails, river access points, libraries, and community organizations (Salt Lake City Planning Division, 2014). Among these many assets are a multitude of food access and assistance programs as well as thriving urban agriculture and local food movements. However, food access is a persistent issue in the Westside where 29% to 33% of residents report experiencing food insecurity (Cabrera, 2022). And, despite a strong community focus on education—particularly evident around community support of the Glendale/Mt View Community Learning Center—educational inequities persist. There is no public high school in the Westside so students are bused across an interstate freeway to predominantly white areas of the city where they report discrimination and a lack of belonging (Cachelin et al., 2022).

### *Food Apartheid*

Several Westside neighborhoods are labeled as "food deserts," a designation popularized by the U.S. Department of Agriculture that refers to an area of widespread food insecurity (Olson, 2018; USDA ERS, 2021). Food insecurity has been defined as a "lack of consistent access to sufficient quality and quantity of food" which poses several risks to human health (Schmeer & Piperata,

2017, p. 1). While the food desert label has gained visibility over the last several years, many scholars point out that the prevalence of food deserts in communities of color suggest this phenomenon may be more aptly described as food apartheid (Holt-Giménez & Harper, 2016; Sbicca, 2012), meaning the systemic production of food inequity through intentional racial and economic policies and practices (Brones, 2018; Reese, 2019). Food apartheid is manifest in many urban areas across the United States where political and economic histories of discrimination combine to produce clusters of food insecurity in communities of color (Lewis, 2018; Reese, 2019; Walker et al., 2010).

As we studied questions of food equity, we noted the overlap between USDA designated food deserts and formerly redlined residential areas in Salt Lake City. Residential redlining was a discriminatory mortgage lending practice through which bankers denied home loans to primarily BIPOC applicants based on racial demographics of particular neighborhoods (Nelson et al., 2020; McClintock, 2011). While the practice was outlawed in 1968, its legacy continues to contribute to racial segregation in many major cities across the United States (Nelson et al., 2020). Using Geographic Information System analysis, we confirmed this pattern is repeated in SLC, where a much higher density of people of color reside in formerly redlined neighborhoods (Joyner, Yagüe, et al., 2022). Figure 9.1 (below) uses 2020 U.S. Census data to illustrate the legacy of redlining practices in Salt Lake City's development and the current concentration of BIPOC communities in Westside neighborhoods.

Map 1 in Figure 9.1 illustrates the concentration of Hispanics and people of color (BIPOC) on a contemporary map of the city. This dot density map represents the Hispanic and non-Hispanic non-white (Black, Asian, American Indian, Alaskan Native, Pacific Islander, and Native Hawaiian) population taken together. The redlining district (category – D in dark gray outlines) overlain on this map helps further illustrate the concentration of Hispanic and BIPOC population within the historically most disadvantaged redline district categorized as "Hazardous" for mortgage and home loan purposes. Additionally, it also illustrates the historical legacy of housing segregation policies like redlining districts where the concentration of people of color and "hazardous" areas coincide on the Westside of Salt Lake City, even in the present time. Map 2 provides a detailed distribution of all four residential historic redlining categories in Salt Lake City. The chart in Figure 9.1 categorized the white and

**Figure 9.1:**
*Concentration of Hispanic and Non-Hispanic BIPOC Population in Salt Lake City, 2020*

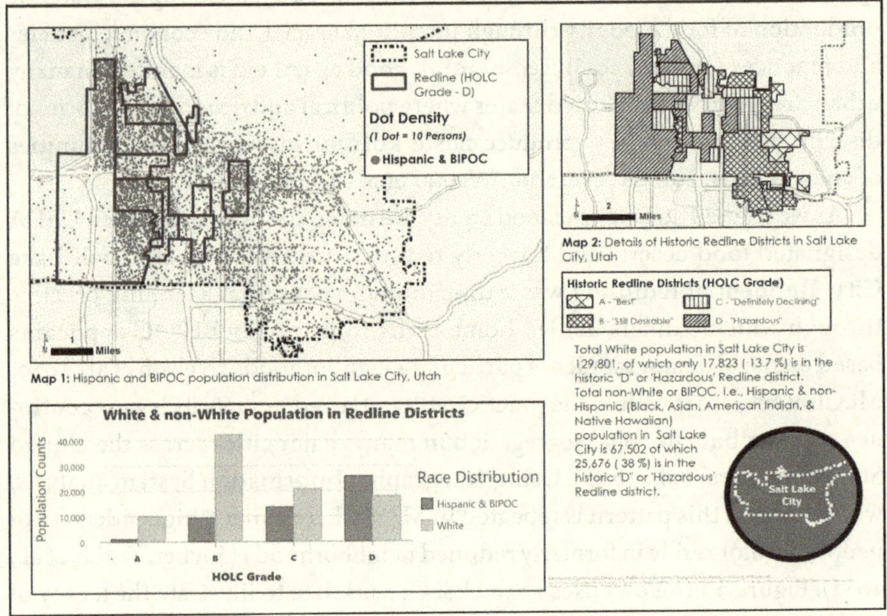


non-white (Hispanic and BIPOC) population for all the districts, demonstrating that the lowest number of Hispanic and BIPOC population resides in the "A" or the "Best" category of the districts. Incidentally, only 13.7% of the white population in Salt Lake City resides in the "D" category of the redline district, whereas 38% of the Hispanic and BIPOC population resides in that same redline category.

A cluster analysis conducted in the ArcGIS software using Anselin's Local Moran Index confirmed that there is statistically significant "High-High" cluster (Moran's Index: 0.29, z-score: 27.39, p-value: 0.00) of Hispanic and BIPOC population in the Westside of Salt Lake. While Moran's Index value depicting clustering of a spatial phenomenon ranges from –1 to +1, in our analysis a Moran's Index of 0.29 with a statistically significant z-score points to the clustering of non-white population on the Westside of the city.

## *Educational Equity*

While some of the author team examined the roots of food injustice in the Westside, other members were simultaneously exploring how these same political and economic legacies shaped educational access. Like other low-wealth communities and communities of color around the country, Westside students experience less expert and lower-paid teachers (Wood, 2015) and have significantly lower rates of college attendance (Byrne, 2018). One structural issue that has come to the forefront of the community's attention is the lack of a Westside high school despite data that reveal where the youth population is highest (Figure 9.2, left).

**Figure 9.2:**
*Distribution of school-aged children (left), percent of Hispanic and BIPOC children in elementary schools (center) and feeder elementary schools (right) in Salt Lake City, 2020*

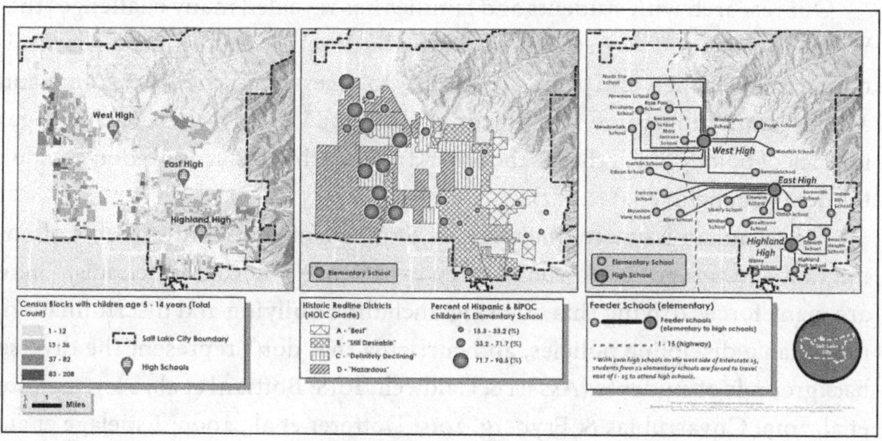


In the Salt Lake City school district as of 2020, over 1,300 Westside students are bused to the Eastside of the city each day, representing over 65% of students at two Eastside high schools (Education Collective SLC, 2020). The map on the left in Figure 9.2 shows the distribution of school-age children (all races) from 5 to 14 years old in Salt Lake City using the 2020 U.S. Census data. It depicts a higher concentration of youth on the Westside, while two out of the only three high schools in the city are on the Eastside. The map in the center (Figure 9.2) illustrates where students of color attend elementary school (proportional gray circles) as a percentage of school attendees. Data from Education Collective SLC (2020) show that Hispanic and non-Hispanic BIPOC students comprise 28% of all students in the three high schools. However, 50% of these students go to the two high schools on the city's Eastside. This illustrates that even with a higher percentage of students of color on the Westside and a higher attendance of them in the Westside elementary schools, they need to travel to the Eastside because of a lack of high schools in the West. This pattern is further explained by the feeder school map (Figure 9.2, right), which clearly shows that children from 12 elementary schools on the Westside must travel across an interstate highway to attend high schools. This map collection was prepared using data from the Salt Lake City School District and the 2020 spatial dataset created in collaboration with the Wasatch Front Regional Council, Utah State Board of Education, and Utah Geospatial Resource Center.

Our research with students and families has revealed many challenges that Westside residents face in their Eastside high schools, including racial discrimination from teachers and peers, an inability to access afterschool programs, and a lack of family engagement (Cachelin et al., 2022). Underlying these challenges is a lack of belonging in these schools and a sense that the schools don't belong to them (Cachelin et al., 2022).

This is not an issue unique to Utah. Students of color and students of immigrant and refugee background often experience othering in schools. There are many forces driving this othering, including bullying and discrimination, inequitable discipline policies, and curricula that don't represent the diverse backgrounds of students (Assari & Caldwell, 2018; Bottiani et al., 2017; Celeste et al, 2019; Covarrubias & Fryberg, 2015; Dotterer et al., 2009; Espelage et al., 2015; He & Fischer, 2020; Morrison et al., 2005; Owens & McLanahan, 2020; Russell et al., 2014). School belonging has been decreasing, on average, around the world over the past 20 years (Avvisati, 2019; OECD, 2023). "Disadvantaged students" report lower levels of belonging than their more advantaged peers (OECD, 2023), and many countries have belonging gaps between wealthy and nonwealthy students, boys and girls, and immigrants and native-born students (OECD, 2019). In other words, "belonging functions as a privilege that adheres to other systemic privileges, rather than a right available to all students" (Kuttner, 2023, p. 1).

## Evolving praxis, challenging assumptions

With a more critical understanding of the systemic patterns of federal and district level zoning and their social legacies, we began to consider the action components of our research. In this section, we begin the process of "marinat[ing] in dialogues about power and difference, divergent interpretations, and a search for new understandings," which is central to critical participatory action research (Fine & Torre, 2021, p. 80). These dialogues allowed us to unpack our assumptions around food justice and educational equity and discuss across our different roles and positionalities, ultimately recognizing our own biases and recalibrating our action research.

### *Voices for Food Sovereignty*

While markers of food apartheid are present in the Westside, so too are resilient community foodways. Here, several neighborhood food retailers exist, and refugee, immigrant, and other community members identify strong foodways and practices connected to traditional foods, cultural identity, and community building (Cachelin et al., 2019). A great deal of food is also grown in Westside small farms and gardens, especially in the Glendale neighborhood where there is a growing urban agriculture movement.

Our team noted a disconnect between the amount of food being grown in the Westside and its availability and affordability there. Urban farmers expressed concern about the possibility that they may be exporting produce to predominantly white and more affluent neighborhoods elsewhere in the city. These concerns were connected to the primarily young white urban farmers' desires to understand their own positionality within their neighborhood and the patterns of food inequity they have noticed across Salt Lake City. This pattern is also related to insights about land values gleaned during our fieldwork, through which both community partners and urban farmers pointed out the pattern of increased availability and lower cost of larger plots of land in the Westside.

This area has attracted young, middle-class, and often white urban farmers to the Westside to access land for farming—a pattern documented in other areas of the United States where redlining has perversely kept development interest low enough to retain the last urban open space for micro-farms nested in food-apartheid impacted communities (Sbicca, 2019). Ultimately, while we see a good amount of food production on the Westside, data suggest not much of that produce is consumed here.

**Figure 9.3:**
*Urban Agriculture in the Glendale Neighborhood*

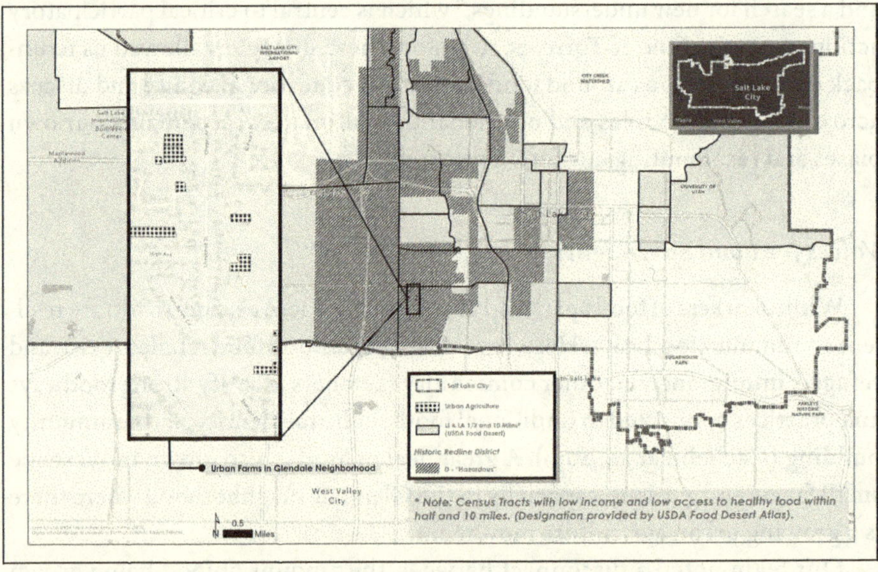


Figure 9.3 above shows the distribution of urban agriculture in the Glendale neighborhood. This Westside neighborhood of Glendale is both food insecure and formerly redlined yet the close-up view shows how many small farms (rectangles with black dots in Figure 9.3) exist there. This area also falls within the USDA-designated food desert (2019 Food Access Research Atlas) showing concentration of low income and low access to healthy food sources within half and 10 miles radius.

Our initial response to data confirming the farmers' export of produce to wealthier areas of the city was to explore subsidized buying options for low-income residents in the Westside. This idea was supported by the majority of one farm's Eastside customers, yet, through continued fieldwork, we learned that similar charity-based approaches had been implemented and failed. We then engaged in a more comprehensive inquiry through dialogue with urban farmers, food access advocates, and Westside residents. In one interview, a representative of a local food access advocacy nonprofit reflected ruefully on a pop-up market their organization launched to promote local food access, saying:

> Most of our funding was based on this idea of making local produce available. And maybe trying to solve both of those problems [hunger & local food production] at the same time was a really big mistake ... What we realized too, was that most of the [sales] of the produce was coming from staff at those centers ... we weren't serving anyone, we were serving mostly people doing food access work.

This food access advocate recognized that because their organization did not design the pop-up market strategy in conjunction with community members, it was largely underutilized. We realized we had almost replicated this dynamic in our own work by suggesting subsidized shares to increase access to local food instead of recognizing where decision-making power must lie. There was more we needed to learn from residents' perspectives. In further investigation, we documented the desire for local, ecologically-sound food systems based in a diversity of land use strategies. We heard from many people that they wanted more active and engaged ways of being involved in the food system, and that didn't necessarily include subsidized models. Many residents shared sentiments like the following quote, in which a community member said, "*I would like to know where my food grows and be more involved so I can learn how to grow it and help more people learn too.*"

As we discovered through interviews and community engagement, residents were interested in more opportunities to grow food. Our partners at one farm told us that many of their neighbors had expressed interest in access to extra seedlings and plants instead of just low-cost produce. We also learned that people were willing to purchase local food, and what they needed was a removal of barriers to growing and buying food instead (see Joyner, Cachelin, et al., 2022). People really wanted active engagement.

This perspective is wholly in keeping with food sovereignty approaches, or "the right of peoples to healthy and culturally appropriate food produced through ecologically sound and sustainable methods, and their right to define their own food and agriculture systems" (Nyéléni, 2007, p. 7). Food sovereignty makes visible the systems of oppression that produce food apartheid and promotes the democratization of food systems in which people, not corporations, are in control (Agyeman & McEntee, 2014; Heynen, 2009; Holt-Giménez & Wang, 2011; Whyte, 2017). Urban agriculture is a critical tool in the pursuit of food sovereignty, as it can increase availability of fresh food in urban centers, promoting health equity, community resilience, and food justice (Alkon & Norgaard, 2009; Angotti, 2015; Dubbeling & de Zeeuw, 2011; Martin et al., 2016). Our research team was reminded that working toward food sovereignty rather than simply food security was at the heart of our work. While we initially considered subsidized farm shares an easy win, we recognized the need to pause and reflect, which was critical to reshaping our thinking and the next steps of our work.

### *Voices for Educational Equity*

Our educational equity team had similar experiences that challenged our assumptions as deeper understandings continued to unfold. With questions about the impacts of busing more than half of the population of East High School from across the city, research collaborators set out to better understand the experience of students from the Glendale area where the population is very diverse: (38.6% Hispanic/Latinx, 35.9% white, 3.9% Black, 10.5% Asian, 1.9% mixed race, and 9.2% other; (U.S. Census Bureau, 2020) as opposed to the area where students were sent (90.6% white) (U.S. Census Bureau, 2020).

Early in the process, a powerful story was shared with the research team that shook our assumptions, giving us insight into what student success should look like. A Westside Tongan student, who some of us had known since 6th grade, came back to visit the Community Learning Center as an adult. He had excelled academically, was a star football player, and had been the student body president. This is someone who was perceived by many as a success story, yet his experience was not one of joy and achievement. Rather, he shared the fact that he never liked football, and throughout his experience as student body president he was told by classmates that if a better-resourced student had held that office, their parents could have provided resources. He hated the experiences. For our research team, this story made us recognize our vision of success was profoundly limiting and misguided. This student knew early on that there was only one societally approved path for a Tongan student in Glendale—that of being a star football player—and many of us have supported that limiting stereotype, thinking we were being encouraging, when what we actually we needed was to forge a more diverse set of possibilities for student success amongst marginalized populations.

To do this, we needed to be able to document student experiences and put different supports in place. This recognition shaped the Glendale Voices research project in which participants were initially recruited through snowball sampling (Atkinson & Flint, 2001). The research team conducted five focus groups with between three and eight participants. Focus groups were conducted by trained facilitators and SPARC Environmental Justice lab staff, many of whom were recruited from the Glendale community. Focus group prompts were open ended so that participants could share experiences in detail and build from each other's ideas. This technique has been recognized as one in which individuals are more likely to provide candid responses (Leung & Savithiri, 2009). Students were asked about impactful experiences, the transition from their home neighborhood to another, and to share perceptions related to how their cultural roots impacted their high school experience so that researchers could better understand both the strengths and challenges of that experience. In this study, we learned that belonging was lacking for students who attended high school outside of the community (their only option) and racialized stereotypes were playing out in some disturbing ways (Cachelin et al., 2022). For example, one student described their experience with one of the teachers:

> *Yeah, she was very stereotypical because she would place all the loud kids in the front row. All the Polys in the front row. 'Cause we were too loud. I am just like what the heck I don't even talk in this class. I was like what the heck is this? Well at least she realized I was Polynesian . . .*

This particular quote illustrates how students are seen and not seen at the same time and was just one example of the ways students described racialized responses from teachers and counselors. Expressions regarding sense of belonging were frequently tied to these racialized stereotypes and were among the most frequently reported overall. Expressions related to belonging include:

> *Just like when you're going up there, like who do you become? Because now you are in a different area, with different people, and it's like trying to be like, it's like when your mom takes you to the store and asks you not to touch anything, you know?*

and, from another participant:

> *. . . like when the teachers are always questioning you, you start thinking, 'maybe I don't belong here, maybe I shouldn't challenge myself.' And you slowly start thinking, like, 'oh I shouldn't shoot for the stars I should just jump a little bit.'*

These comments provide insight into how incredibly damaging the lack of belonging can be beyond just academic achievement. Here we see students hesitant to strive and fully engage in the school community. Further, we hear students questioning their own value and self-worth as their identities are shaped.

In addition to gaining understanding about the experience of belonging, creating space for people to talk has been valuable—simply expressing their ideas and having them validated was powerful. Intentionally supporting community focus group facilitators to be a part of this research project was an important element of our praxis. These facilitators held lived experiences relating directly to the project, allowing us to build a deeper understanding of existing barriers and to create opportunities for participants to build networks and relationships with community leaders. Beyond gathering data that can support better decision making and hold policymakers accountable, we noted the ways our praxis supported additional community-driven organizing efforts. These conversations sparked the possibility that youth and families can organize, make demands, and take up space to make sure they have what is needed and wanted as a community. In fact, this work has been used to support the Education Collective SLC in their request to the superintendent for a community-based school on the Westside. This dialogue is ongoing.

At the same time, our team was committed to expanding what success could look like for minoritized students and how we could create nonathletic pathways to higher education.

## Dream convergence

We couldn't help but wonder how we might find an integrative approach to challenge these inequities and work towards justice. The Growing Educational Pathways for Food Sovereignty (GEPFS) program is that approach. This program engages students from food apartheid–impacted communities who are bused out of their neighborhoods for high school in an attempt to foster belonging in both community and university settings, while producing food and learning about urban agriculture.

We are building on existing research establishing that community garden programs, culturally responsive/sustaining pedagogies, and family engagement can engender student belonging (Borck, 2020; Guitart et al., 2012; Osterman, 2000). At the same time, we are expanding beyond narrow definitions of school belonging, which frame this construct as primarily a psychological phenomenon (e.g., Goodenow & Grady, 1993). Belonging is not just a "sense": for students of color and students of immigrant and refugee background, navigating school belonging is a complex social, cultural, and even political process. Our work draws on a new, critical, transdisciplinary framework called *the right to belong in school* (Kuttner, 2023).

The GEPFS program integrates innovative approaches to promote belonging through cascading mentorship (Afghani et al., 2013), place-based campus–community partnerships (Yamamura & Koth, 2018), and an emphasis on students-as-leaders focused on an issue of import to their families and communities. The program includes several components—an afterschool course for middle schoolers, a high school course for college credit, a paid garden stewards program for graduates of the previous program cohorts who go on to attend the University of Utah, and finally current students and future students can work together in the SPARC lab. In this way, we have a model for promoting youth agency through a variety of phases in which students can shape community-level food initiatives. Constructed to highlight community strengths and a diversity of foodways, the course instructors include folks from the university and community, including parents who lead cooking/gardening classes with ingredients harvested from the garden.

We launched the pilot of the high school course with a group of nine students from the Westside. What was exciting about having such a small group of students was that we got to work with them to shape the curriculum ahead of the class. They told us that they wanted to learn about gardening, about cooking, and about how their own cultural foodways take shape. The course happened in several different locations with a home base at the Glendale Mt.-View Community Learning Center Garden. We also visited the campus gardens at the University of Utah each week, and various urban farms and gardens around Salt Lake City. We hoped not only to foster belonging in gardens on campuses but also to investigate different ways that urban agriculture takes place given differential commitments to food sovereignty based in critical theory.

When we asked students about some of their major takeaways from the course they noted:

> *. . . starting your own garden and managing it isn't as hard as I imagined, since you don't need a lot of money or space to start one, even if it is small or not that great looking. You can learn and improve in the future*

> *industrial agriculture . . . reaps short-term benefits . . . depletes our resources and minimizes seed diversity. I also learned how to grow herbs in a small pot.*

> *I learn[ed] there are many simple ways we can grow our own food without needing to constantly go to stores. We visited many neighbors in Glendale who had implemented gardens in places one wouldn't even think of. And these gardens are very good in comparison to industrial agriculture . . .*

> *There are many consequences that come from [gardening], and if we could all learn to implement the same ideas we learned [in] the community in our own personal lives, we could not only have more accessible food for ourself, but also have a small part in stopping the damage on the environment.*

These responses, reflecting both disillusionment with industrial agriculture and the skills and interest in growing food suggest that our hopes of increasing food sovereignty and educational equity are possible. And we see the development of a right to belong. We are exploring the possibilities for the GEPFS model to be impactful in a variety of community settings; we have identified Sacramento California as a location to launch a sister-site due to its recognition as "America's Farm-to-Fork Capital" where food insecurity is also a persistent issue (Joyner et al., 2023). In keeping with the commitments to community-engaged research, we are launching this project with a phase of exploratory fieldwork to establish relationships with community members, form an initial understanding of the local foodscape, build relationships, and explore the unique community context. In this initial phase, we are building opportunities for critical reflection into our interview methodologies (Joyner et al., 2023) and expect that through interviews designed to explore community members' dreams and visions we might uncover other opportunities and needs. This approach centers on one of the most important lessons we have learned from this project: that community-engaged work is necessarily iterative and creates possibilities and outcomes that cannot be identified in advance.

## Listening as research in the social change journey

Embracing social change as iterative and nonlinear, as a process not a product, has been central to the current rendering of the GEPFS project. As adrienne maree brown (2017) reminds us, ". . . in a non-linear process, everything is part of the learning, every step, this includes constructive criticism—it is a part of the feedback loop—experiment, gather feedback, experiment again" (p. 106). As a collaborative we have had ideas and assumptions tested and reshaped throughout our project and have valued unlearning and relearning from these processes. As Rebecca Solnit (2016) reminds us, "*Hope locates itself in the premises that we don't know what will happen and that in the spaciousness of uncertainty there is space to act*" (p. xiv).

Through our journey we have recognized that community work doesn't have a clear endpoint; rather, continued dialogue, reflection, and evolving initiatives are both journey and destination. Through this lens, detours and even roadblocks are both natural and generative in that they require collaborators to dig deeper and become more creative. This approach is not only consistent with a variety of social movement theory (see McAdam & Tarrow, 2018) but also resonates with critiques of traditional Western research that has been indicted as extractive and short term. Thus, the tools of analysis in long-term partnerships may best be aligned with valuing evolving goals, ongoing co-construction of knowledge, and reciprocity. In the end, the outcomes of community-engaged research may look entirely different than anticipated and, given interconnected roots, may provide for the convergence of several initiatives. It is precisely that spirit that drives the process of critical participatory action research (Fine & Torre, 2021) as an evolving and transformative practice.

## References

Afghani, B., Santos, R., Angulo, M., & Muratori, W. (2013). A novel enrichment program using cascading mentorship to increase diversity in the health care professions. *Academic Medicine, 88*(9), 1232–1238. https://doi.org/10.1097/ACM.0b013e31829ed47e

Agyeman, J., & McEntee, J. (2014). Moving the field of food justice forward through the lens of urban political ecology. *Geography Compass, 8*, 211–220. https://doi.org/10.1111/gec3.12122.

Alkon, A., & Norgaard, K. (2009). Breaking the food chains: An investigation of food justice activism. *Sociological Inquiry, 79*(3), 289–305. https://doi.org/10.1111/j.1475-682X.2009.00291.x

Angotti, T. (2015). Urban agriculture: long-term strategy or impossible dream?: Lessons from prospect farm in Brooklyn, New York. *Public Health, 129*(4), 336–341. https://doi.org/10.1016/j.puhe.2014.12.008

Assari, S., & Caldwell, C. H. (2018). Teacher discrimination reduces school performance of African American youth: role of gender. *Brain Sciences, 8*(10), 183. https://doi.org/10.3390/brainsci8100183

Atkinson, R., & Flint, J. (2001). Accessing hidden and hard-to-reach populations: Snowball research strategies. *Social Research Update, 33*(1), 1–4.

Avvisati, F. (2019). *Have students' feelings of belonging at school waned over time?* PISA in focus #100. OECD.

Borck, C. (2020). "I belong here.": Culturally sustaining pedagogical praxes from an alternative high school in Brooklyn. *The Urban Review, 52*(2), 376–391.

Bottiani, J. H., Bradshaw, C. P., & Mendelson, T. (2017). A multilevel examination of racial disparities in high school discipline: Black and white adolescents' perceived equity, school belonging, and adjustment problems. *Journal of Educational Psychology, 109*(4), 532. https://doi.org/10.1037/edu0000155

Brones, A. (2018, May 7). Karen Washington: It's not a food desert, it's food apartheid. *Guernica*. https://www.guernicamag.com/karen-washington-its-not-a-food-desert-its-food-apartheid/

brown, a. m. (2017). *Emergent strategy: Shaping change, changing worlds.* AK Press.

Byrne, K. (2018). *University Neighborhood Partners Annual Report: May 2017-April 2018.* University Neighborhood Partners, University of Utah.

Cabrera, A. (2022). Food inequality haunts SLC's west side. Here's how residents are working to change that. *Salt Lake Tribune*. https://www.sltrib.com/news/2022/02/22/food-inequality-haunts/

Cachelin, A., Christian, P., & Goeckeritz, K. (2022). Glendale voices: Understanding student perspectives on the high school experience. SPARC Environmental Justice Lab. Salt Lake City, UT.

Cachelin, A., Ivkovich, L., Jensen, P., & Neild, M. (2019). Leveraging foodways for health and justice. *Local Environment, 24*(5), 417–427. https://doi.org/10.1080/13549839.2019.1585771

Celeste, L., Baysu, G., Phalet, K., Meeussen, L., & Kende, J. (2019). Can school diversity policies reduce belonging and achievement gaps between minority and majority youth? Multiculturalism, colorblindness, and assimilationism assessed. *Personality and Social Psychology Bulletin, 45*(11), 1603–1618. https://doi.org/10.1177/0146167219838577

Covarrubias, R., & Fryberg, S. A. (2015). The impact of self-relevant representations on school belonging for Native American students. *Cultural Diversity and Ethnic Minority Psychology, 21*(1), 10. https://doi.org/10.1037/a0037819

Denzin, N. K., & Lincoln, Y. S. (2018). *The SAGE handbook of qualitative research* (5th ed., pp. 195–213). SAGE.

Dotterer, A. M., McHale, S. M., & Crouter, A. C. (2009). Sociocultural factors and school engagement among African American youth: The roles of racial discrimination, racial socialization, and ethnic identity. *Applied Development Science, 13*(2), 61–73.

Dubbeling, M., & de Zeeuw, H. (2011). Urban agriculture and climate change adaptation: ensuring food security through adaptation. In: Otto-Zimmermann K (Ed.), *Resilient cities* (pp. 441–449). Dordrecht. http://doi.org/10.1007/978-94-007-0785-6

Education Collective SLC. (2020, December 10). Community request letter. Education Collective SLC. https://www.edcollectiveslc.org/_files/ugd/29d2d4_9670b22e847842cab51342922f9c2e50.pdf?index=true

Espelage, D. L., Hong, J. S., Rao, M. A., & Thornberg, R. (2015). Understanding ecological factors associated with bullying across the elementary to middle school transition in the United States. *Violence and Victims, 30*, 470–487. https://doi.org/10.1891/0886-6708.VV-D-14-00046

Fine, M., & Torre, M. E. (2021). *Essentials of critical participatory action research*. American Psychological Association.

Goodenow, C., & Grady, K. E. (1993). The relationship of school belonging and friends' values to academic motivation among urban adolescent students. *The Journal of Experimental Education, 62*(1), 60–71.

Guitart, D., Pickering, C. & Byrne, J., (2012). Past results and future directions in urban community gardens research. *Urban Forestry & Urban Greening, 11*(4), 364–373.

He, J., & Fischer, J. (2020). Differential associations of school practices with achievement and sense of belonging of immigrant and non-immigrant students. *Journal of Applied Developmental Psychology, 66*, 101089. https://doi.org/10.1016/j.appdev.2019.101089

Heynen, N. (2009). Bending the bars of empire from every ghetto for survival: The Black Panther Party's radical antihunger politics of social reproduction and scale. *Annals of the Association of American Geographers, 99*(2), 406–422. https://doi.org/10.1080/00045600802683767

Holt-Giménez, E., & Harper, B. (2016). Food systems racism: From mistreatment to transformation. *Food First, 1*(2), 1–7.

Holt-Giménez, E., & Wang, Y. (2011). Reform or transformation? The pivotal role of food justice in the US food movement. *Race/Ethnicity: Multidisciplinary Global Contexts*, 5, 83–102. https://doi.org/10.2979/racethmulglocon.5.1.83

Joyner, L., Cachelin, A., & Yagüe, B. (2022). Increasing food sovereignty: Insights from Salt Lake City farmers and food advocates. Research summary and report prepared for SPARC Environmental Justice Lab, Salt Lake City, UT. University of Utah. https://sparc.utah.edu/outcomes-and-impacts/index.php

Joyner, L., Yagüe, B., Cachelin, A., & Rose, J. (2022). Farms and gardens everywhere but not a bite to eat? A critical geographic approach to food apartheid in Salt Lake City. *Journal of Agriculture, Food Systems, and Community Development, 11*(2), 67–88. https://doi.org/10.5304/jafscd.2022.112.013

Joyner, L., Yagüe, B., & Cachelin, C. (2023). Promoting food systems paradigm shifts through critical reflexivity: Exploring interviews as intervention. *Social Sciences, 12*, 280. https://doi.org/10.3390/socsci12050280

Kuttner, P. J. (2023). The right to belong in school: A critical, transdisciplinary conceptualization of school belonging. AERA Open, 9. https://doi-org.ezproxy.lib.utah.edu/10.1177/23328584231183407

Leung, F. H., & Savithiri, R. (2009). Spotlight on focus groups. *Canadian Family Physician, 55*(2), 218–219.

Lewis, D. (2018). Gender, feminism and food studies: A critical review. *African Security Review, 24*(4), 414–429. https://doi.org/10.1080/10246029.2015.1090115

Martin, G., Clift, R., & Christie, I. (2016). Urban cultivation and its contributions to sustainability: Nibbles of food but oodles of social capital. *Sustainability, 8*(5), 409. https://doi.org/10.3390/su8050409

McAdam, D., and Tarrow, S. (2018). The political context of social movements. In D. A. Snow, S. A. Soule, H. Kriesi, & H. J. McCammon (Eds.), *The Wiley Blackwell companion to social movements*. https://doi-org.ezproxy.lib.utah.edu/10.1002/9781119168577.ch1

McClintock, N. (2011). From industrial garden to food desert. In A. Alkon & J. Agyeman (Eds.), *Cultivating food justice: Race, class, and sustainability* (pp. 89–120). The MIT Press.

Morrison, B., Blood, P., & Thorsborne, M. (2005). Practicing restorative justice in school communities: Addressing the challenge of culture change. *Public Organization Review, 5*(4), 335–357. https://doi.org/10.1007/s11115-005-5095-6

Nelson, R. K., LaDale, W., Marciano, R., & Connolly, N. (2020). Mapping inequality. In R. K. Nelson & E. L. Ayers (Eds.), *American Panorama*. https://dsl.richmond.edu/panorama/redlining/index.html#loc=3/41.245/-105.469

Nyéléni. (2007). *Nyéléni Forum for Food Sovereignty Declaration*. https://nyeleni.org/DOWNLOADS/Nyelni_EN.pdf

OECD. (2019), PISA 2018 Results (Volume III): *What School Life Means for Students' Lives*, PISA, OECD Publishing. https://doi.org/10.1787/acd78851-en.

OECD. (2023). *PISA 2022 results: Learning during – and from – disruption*. Publication Volume II. OECD Publishing. http://dx.doi.org/10.1787/9789264273856-en

Olson, L. (2018). Great west food desert: City seeks to improve food options on Westside. *Utah Stories*. https://utahstories.com/2018/06/great-west-food-desert-city-seeks-to-improve-food-options-on-westside/

Osterman, K. F. (2000). Students' need for belonging in the school community. *Review of Educational Research, 70*(3), 323–367.

Owens, J., & McLanahan, S. S. (2020). Unpacking the drivers of racial disparities in school suspension and expulsion. *Social Forces, 98*(4), 1548–1577. https://doi.org/10.1093/sf/soz095

Reese, A. M. (2019). *Black food geographies: Race, self-reliance, and food access in Washington, D.C.* The University Of North Carolina Press. https://doi.org/10.5149/northcarolina/9781469651507.001.0001

Reynolds, K., Block, D. R., Hammelman, C., Jones, B. D., Gilbert, J. L., & Herrera, H. (2020). Envisioning radical food geographies: shared learning and praxis through the Food Justice Scholar-Activist/Activist-Scholar Community of Practice. *Human Geography, 13*(3), 277–292. https://doi-org.ezproxy.lib.utah.edu/10.1177/1942778620951934

Russell, S. T., Toomey, R. B., Ryan, C., & Diaz, R. M. (2014). Being out at school: The implications for school victimization and young adult adjustment. *American Journal of Orthopsychiatry, 84*, 635–643. https://doi.org/10.1037/ort0000037

Salt Lake City Planning Division. (2014). *West Side Master Plan*. http://www.slcdocs.com/Planning/MasterPlansMaps/WSLMPA.pdf

Savin-Baden, M., & Major, C. H. (2013). *Qualitative research: The essential guide to theory and practice*. Routledge.

Sbicca, J. (2012). Growing food justice by planting an anti-oppression foundation: Opportunities and obstacles for a budding social movement. *Agriculture and Human Values, 29*(4), 455–466. https://doi.org/10.1007/s10460-012-9363-0

Sbicca, J. (2019). Urban agriculture, revalorization, and green gentrification in Denver, Colorado. In T. Bartley (Ed.), *The politics of land* (pp. 149–170). Emerald Publishing. https://doi.org/10.1108/S0895-993520190000026011

Schmeer, K. K., & Piperata, B. A. (2017). Household food insecurity and child health. *Maternal & Child Nutrition, 13*(2), e12301. https://doi.org/10.1111/mcn.12301

Solnit, R. (2016). *Hope in the dark: Untold histories, wild possibilities.* 3rd ed., Haymarket Books.

University Neighborhood Partners. (2019). *Neighborhoods.* https://partners.utah.edu/about-unp/neighborhoods/

U.S. Census Bureau. (2020). Hispanic or Latino, and Not Hispanic or Latino by Race. Decennial Census, DEC Redistricting Data (PL 94-171), Table P2. Retrieved August 09, 2023, from https://data.census.gov/table/DECENNIALPL2020.P2?q=P2:HISPANIC OR LATINO, AND NOT HISPANIC OR LATINO BYRACE&g=050XX00US49035$1500000

U.S. Department of Agriculture Economic Research Service. (2021). Food access research atlas. https://www.ers.usda.gov/data-products/food-access-research-atlas/

Walker, R. E., Keane, C. R., & Burke, J. G. (2010). Disparities and access to healthy food in the United States: A review of food deserts literature. *Health & Place, 16*(5), 876–884. https://doi.org/10.1016/j.healthplace.2010.04.013

Whyte, K. P. (2017). Indigenous food sovereignty, renewal and US settler colonialism. In M. Rawlinson & C. Ward (Eds.), *The Routledge Handbook of Food Ethics* (pp. 354–365). Routledge.

Wood, B. (2015, October). Turnover and staffing lead to less experienced teachers on SLC's west side. *Salt Lake Tribune.* https://archive.sltrib.com/article.php?id=3010348&itype=CMSID

Yamamura, E. K., & Koth, K. (2018). *Place-based community engagement in higher education: A strategy to transform universities and communities.* Stylus Publishing, LLC.

**Afterword**

# Collaborative Research and Seeking Truth in the Struggle for Justice and Democracy

*Ronald David Glass*

I appreciate the honor of an Afterword and the opportunity to learn from these illuminating chapters. Each one speaks to the transformations made possible, in university courses and in community projects, when seeking truth, collaborative research is put to work in struggles for justice. These transformations support the daily practices of living otherwise than as prescribed by the dominant orders that extend historical injustices through their ordinary commonsense routines and logics; they thus provide bulwarks against the multiple forms of both subtle and flagrant violence that continue to pervade everyday life. The testimonies, stories, and analyses shared in these chapters reveal how to use truth seeking to hold space in the present for accurately depicted pasts and alternative brighter futures; these words have already spoken beyond themselves not only through the material and psychosocial impacts they describe but also through the retellings offered here. I am grateful to receive what is told here.

This Afterword steps into this historical-cultural intergenerational conversation, one with neither first nor last words, only middle words that form the logics of the work for justice and democracy, middle words that grow in volume as long traditions become newly meaningful in the voices of continually added generations. I accept my responsibility as an elder to be asked to listen and respond to the generations now speaking; if I hear truly, I might gain the heights of their visions and feel the depths of their insights for a vantage point through my own decades of particular experiences.

This powerful collection of voices documents the power of learning and knowledge production to transform the self-understanding those seeking to know as well as the limiting social conditions of the lives of those with little social, economic, or political power.

In the first section, *Teaching and Curriculum as Activism,* I hear the intensity and urgency in the voices of Mimi Ghosh, Zenia Lakhani, Alexis Mullard, and Taylor Valci as they speak of new generations coming into their adulthood facing global scale challenges. I hear how strategically co-designed college courses can be geared into long-term ongoing partnerships with movement and labor organizations, with class work focused on specific real-time knowledge production needs of the working class. I am reminded of how my colleagues Steve McKay, Rebecca London, and Miriam Greenberg made community-initiated student-engaged research foundational for enduring partnerships that leveraged student and university resources and knowledge production capacities to co-generate and enact public policies serving the least advantaged in the community—all while providing a wide range of students with profound life-changing experiences that often enable them to "give back" to their communities at the same time as they gained the privilege of a higher education (Greenberg et al., 2020). The testimony in these opening chapters illuminates the ways in which the learning processes of research for justice can themselves be deeply generative, independently of the power of the research findings, outcomes, or products to do their own work in the world.

In the second and third sections, *Community-Based Research as Social Justice* and *Policy and/or Networking as Justice Work,* we see more examples of how the URBAN network of engaged scholars leverage the deeper insights of equity oriented collaborative community-based research as well as institutional power to extend the reach of the work. Angela Frusciante reminds us how knowledge work intersects with philanthropic initiatives, and that a common ground of meaning making allows for interventions that can widen the scope of organizational and programmatic engagement with communities and with their insights and knowledge. This inter/transdisciplinary understanding of knowledge generation, embracing the humanities along with the social sciences, has been central to URBAN since its inception (Warren and Glass, 2019); similarly, URBAN has had a central focus on relational ethics and the actual inter-personal relationships that are the daily stuff of collaborations and partnerships

(Glass et al, 2018). These commitments get revealed in May Lin's report of a participatory research project in which youth leaders demonstrate an intersectional depth of understanding of race and education to design and conduct sophisticated research that supported a statewide campaign for racial justice that demanded schools that care and that foster healthy relationships. The power of truth-seeking working in people and in the world becomes evident.

More and more we are understanding how attention to these primary human needs for respect, love, care, and community that the youth are demanding are just as fundamental to research, to seeking truth, to struggles for justice, as they are fundamental to their schools, to an ethical life, to our ethical practice as scholars.

In fact, it is also essential to bring within the scope of attention all the other-than-human relations in which we and our work are embedded, with the land, water, and air and all that walks, crawls, slithers, swims, and flies. Becoming attuned to these broader relations, and grounding and leading the work from values, is integral to Indigenous approaches to equity research as elaborated here by Morgan Love, Kathleen Knight, Jonnie Williams, and Marcos Vargas.

As these engaged scholars of the URBAN network grapple with the many forms of violence and injustice pervading everyday life, it becomes evident that this requires developing insightful investigations to help understand ourselves and our world and the inequitable limits imposed on us, and it requires shaping strategic action plans to combat entrenched worldly powers backed by economic, police, and military force, and, at the same time, it requires that we heal from historical and ongoing trauma so that we can achieve the clarity needed to make deep and lasting change.

When we grasp the depths to which this healing must reach and the ways in which injustice plays out in the lives of all of us, we begin to understand not just the need for compassionate intergenerational learning and work, but multigenerational strategies that begin with the youngest among us. Paige Bray and Erin Kenney inspire us with the structural changes that became possible when their work scaled from the local to the global and across generations within values-informed partnerships that amplified equitable best practices for the critical education of young children and their care givers. Here again we witness the crucial importance of building on the ground of inclusion and equity so that participation and learning enable people and organizations to stay energized and make present more of the freedom dreams and aspirations that point beyond the limiting conditions they must confront.

It seems fitting that this inspiring and powerful collection closes with "Embracing the Journey," which situates collaborative knowledge production in the struggle for educational justice and food sovereignty, and in the critical hope that is sustained through those struggles themselves. This exceptional project—multigenerational, multivocal, and multifaceted; historically attuned, locally grounded, globally aligned, and future oriented—is brought to life for us by co-authors Adrienne Cachelin, Leah Joyner, Paul Kuttner, Gilberto Rejon Magana, Elizabeth Montoya, Jarred Martinez, Keri Taddie, Blanca Yagüe, and Debolina Banerjee.

Here we witness the power of growing equity from the ground up, of drawing on the fertile capacities and resources at hand that the dominant powers marginalize, and of refusing the seemingly ordained fates of food deserts and circumscribed educational and life opportunities. Again and again these chapters show us the power of projects in critical learning to know better the situation of our lives and thus to reveal the actions needed and within reach that can transform injustice.

The voices in these chapters speak as one in demonstrating that when critical truth-seeking is set to work through collaborative research for justice, then individual lives, organizations, institutions, and communities can be transformed for the better. These learning and knowledge generation processes extend to involve wider circles of people, each circle growing more critical consciousness concerning the possibilities of their lives, and at the same time forging more social, cultural, and political power that opens paths forward to achieve their dreams of a more just and democratic society. This is how critical knowledge is fused with critical hope in the body of movements that make and remake history.

Now, at a time when truth itself is in crisis, it is clear that we must redouble efforts to support collaborative approaches to community–university partnerships aimed at truly equitably co-creating knowledge for justice. Scholars and students from across the disciplinary spectrum, community organizers and leaders, foundation program officers and board members, artists, activists, and regular folks need to widen every opening for collaborative action research to be able to respond to the fraught conditions created when lies and misinformation pervade the discourse that circulates most rapidly and widely. It is a time when we have to be All In to withstand and confront open assaults on the very possibility of the value of truth seeking.

Thankfully, the URBAN network, with footholds in a variety of institutional spaces scattered across the United States, is not the only center of innovation and support for this work and new generations of engaged scholars. The Institute for Social Transformation at the University of California, Santa Cruz, the Public Science Project at the Graduate Center at the City University of New York also incubate interdisciplinary, cross sectoral, intergenerational critical participatory community based research projects and programs. But as we know from long and often bitter experience, these openings and institutional spaces can be quickly closed, and so we learn to stay alive and do the work regardless, somehow, some way. With leading national research funders like Robert Wood Johnson, Spencer, and WT Grant foundations, and the National Science Foundation, now recognizing the reach and rigor of collaborative community-based research, more support is becoming available at a crucial moment.

The URBAN community of scholars, researchers, policy advocates, community leaders, educators, and students will continue to face an environment of both opportunity and opposition. The opportunities, as always, emerge from need and necessity. The opposition emerges from both the expected and long-contested inertias that academic and community organizing traditions have presented to collaborative, community-based research for justice. More pointedly, the opposition emerges from the rise of an unprecedented neo-fascist political movement in the United States that is committed to a resurrection and resuscitation of patriarchal white supremacy and thus has launched sustained attacks on all people and things that can be attached to "social justice, diversity, equity, and inclusion" initiatives in education. As already noted, these attacks have been mounted on the ground of sustained assaults on truth itself, on the manufacture of misinformation, disinformation, and bullshit (Frankfurt, 2005), thus creating a crisis in the epistemological foundations of the society, deepening the fractures and opening possibilities for exploitation by malevolent forces seeking authoritarian control.

This present context seems to require that university-based community-engaged scholars stand at a leading edge of the cultural, ethical, and political response to these threats to democracy and to justice. This demand is derived from the fact that in the crisis of truth, those forms of knowledge production that are equitable, collaborative, and community-engaged are those that are best positioned to do three interwoven things:

1. establish credible forms of warrant for the evidence and arguments that yield rigorous knowledge and that is recognized inside and outside of academe;
2. make research processes also community-based learning processes that systematically develop, share, and disseminate knowledge in multiple relevant forms that draw from a wider set of experiences and extend the reach of the findings; and
3. ensure impact and transformations toward justice and democracy by integrating knowledge dissemination and mobilization through critical learning processes that also build social/political power.

Perhaps it is not too much hyperbole to say that the future of democratic societies and struggles for justice may very well depend on the success of the efforts to build and extend the field of equity oriented collaborative community based research. Based on the inspiring accounts shared in this collection, I think if we go All In, the field will be up to the task!

## References:

Frankfurt, H. G. (2005). *On Bullshit.* Princeton University Press.

Glass, R.D., Morton, J.,King, J.E., Krueger-Henney,P., Moses, M.S., Sabati, S.,Richardson, T. 2018. The Ethical Stakes of Collaborative Community-Based Research. *Urban Education,* 53(4), 503–531.

Greenberg, M., London, R. A., & McKay, S. C. (2020). Community-initiated student-engaged research: Expanding undergraduate teaching and learning through public sociology. *Teaching Sociology, 48*(1), 13–27. https://doi.org/10.1177/0092055X19875794

Warren, M. R., & Glass, R. D. (2019). Collaborative research and multi-issue movement building for educational justice: Reflections on the Urban Research Based Action Network (URBAN). *Education Policy Analysis Archives,* 27, 53. https://doi.org/10.14507/epaa.27.4445

## About the Authors

**Ana Carolina Antunes** (she/her) is an Assistant Professor in the Division of Gender Studies at the University of Utah and the lead co-chair of the Urban Research-Based Action Network. Her work focuses on community-engaged research and critical youth and refugee studies. Her current research project investigates the intersection of comprehensive sexuality education and culturally relevant pedagogy and its effects on youth self-perception.

**Debolina Banerjee, Ph.D.**, is a Postdoctoral Research Fellow in the SPARC Environmental Justice Lab at the University of Utah. Her work has focused on the human dimension of urban environmental sustainability, specifically, the social and behavioral drivers that propel higher adoption of climate mitigation strategies like sustainable stormwater technologies. Her research philosophy is influenced by three core concepts—participatory planning integrating local knowledge, human-nature interactions, and socio-psychological theories lending a lens into the perceptual drivers of pro-environmental behaviors. In her current role as a postdoctoral researcher, she is increasingly focused on the nexus between urban ecology and environmental justice & equity. Her primary research interest is at the intersection of complex human-nature interaction in the built environment, and she has investigated issues surrounding water quality, air pollution, vehicular emissions, urban greening, racial segregation, and homelessness through her past and current research projects. As a mixed-method researcher, she extensively uses statistical models, agent-based models, spatial analysis, and qualitative methods in her research projects. As an interdisciplinary researcher trained as a geographer and environmental planner, she integrates urban sustainability's spatial and policy perspective through her research endeavor.

**Paige Bray** is currently an Associate Professor of Early Childhood Education and Center for Montessori Studies Director; three decades of work with allies has addressed systemic inequities. Her teaching expertise in personal "reflexes" and professional identity transitions fosters dynamic inquiry and using meta-cognitive tools across the teaching career continuum. An activist scholar, her research is grounded by community and human capacity as knowledge producers. Her MEd is from Sarah Lawrence College and her EdD is from the University of Massachusetts, Amherst.

**Adrienne Cachelin** is an Associate Professor in Environmental & Sustainability Studies and Geography at the University of Utah. Her research, teaching, and service are integrated and mutually reinforcing, conducted in collaboration with community partners and students in the SPARC Environmental Justice Lab that she directs. Using a critical participatory action framework, Adrienne seeks to ameliorate environmental injustices with a particular interest in urban agriculture.

**Jose Calderon** - Received his A. A. degree from Northeastern Jr. College in Sterling, Colorado; B. A. in Communications from the University of Colorado, Boulder; M. A. and Ph.D in Sociology from the University of California, Los Angeles. He has had a long history as an organic intellectual: connecting his academic work with community organizing, student-based service learning, participatory action research, multi-ethnic coalition-building, and critical pedagogy. He has been at Pitzer College since 1991.

**Angela K. Frusciante, PhD,** is principal of Knowledge Designs to Change, an equity-focused strategy and research practice. As a socio-political scholar, Angela brings over 20 years of experience working in qualitative inquiry across the nonprofit, academic, and philanthropic sectors. Angela is a vetted member of the National Coalition of Independent Scholars and an alumna of the Council on Foundations Career Pathways program. She has served as an author and reviewer for The Foundation Review, the first peer-reviewed journal of philanthropy.

**Mimi Ghosh** - Born and raised in the San Francisco Bay Area, Mimi Ghosh has centered her work around Critical Service Learning. With her background as a South Asian woman, she brings an intersectional feminist perspective to social justice spaces. She holds a B.A. in Humanities and Communication with a concentration in Legal Studies and a minor in Social Justice and Community Leadership. She attended Cal State University Monterey Bay where she worked as a Service Learning Student Leader teaching social justice classes throughout her undergraduate career. In 2022 she captivated audiences at her Capstone Festival with her South Asian Oral History Collective; it was an analysis of a series of interviews she collected capturing the beauty and cultural issues of the female Indian-American immigrant experience through an intergenerational lens. Alongside her work teaching undergraduate students about feminism, homelessness, and service learning, she has presented workshops at social justice conferences at top California universities including UC Berkeley, UC Santa Cruz, and Cal Poly San Luis Obispo. Covering a range of topics, Mimi has presented on decriminalizing homelessness, prison abolition, and rights for Native American, Alaska Native, and Native Hawai'ian women.

**Ronald David Glass** is Professor of Philosophy of Education, emeritus, at the University of California, Santa Cruz; he is a 'kind of historico-cultural-political-psychoanalyst' who has helped facilitate projects in education as a practice of freedom with a wide range of justice-oriented movement and community-based organizations, and with schools, colleges and universities seeking to build a just democracy. He directed (2009-2015) the Center for Collaborative Research for an Equitable California, a University of California Office of the President multi-campus state-wide research program initiative to support interdisciplinary equity-oriented collaborative community-based research, and he has served in the national leadership of URBAN since its inaugural year (2011). His recent work focuses on the ethical issues in research, particularly when truth seeking and knowledge production are geared into efforts to transform oneself and the world toward visions of justice and of human dignity and freedom. Professor Glass has been recognized with numerous honors, including awards for distinguished teaching from both the Stanford University School of Education and the University of California Santa Cruz Division of Social Sciences, and including multiple awards for contributions to racial justice from Arizona State University as well as the City of Phoenix Human Relation Commission's Martin Luther King, Jr. Living the Dream Award (2001). He is the proud and happy father of three people and grandfather of seven more, and resides on unceded Ohlone land, a place also known as Berkeley, CA., where he tends his small garden and greets each day with gratitude.

**Joy Howard** is an Associate Professor in the Human Services Department at Western Carolina University. Her work focuses on leadership for constructing humanizing educational communities. She is especially interested in humanizing movements and space making, shared and subversive leadership, and beloved communities within a racist society.

**Leah Joyner, PhD** is an Assistant Professor at California State University, Sacramento in the Recreation, Parks, & Tourism Administration program. Her work centers on community-based research regarding issues in environmental justice, food apartheid, and food sovereignty. She has over ten years of experience working in collaborative, community engaged approaches to food and environmental justice. In addition to co-launching the SPARC Environmental Justice Lab at the University of Utah she is also a part of a interdisciplinary team working to identify initiatives to promote food justice and educational equity through experiential education and recreational experiences in urban agriculture in Sacramento. She enjoys spending time outdoors cycling, hiking with her rescue dog, and enjoying ocean or river views with her family and friends.

**Erin Kenney** spent the last two decades as a practitioner working in early care and education settings. Dr. Kenney is committed to interdisciplinary work. She earned her MEd in early childhood education and PhD in developmental psychology. Her work bridges the gap between developmental science and developmentally appropriate practice. A fulltime faculty member in psychology, she also serves as a program development/evaluation fellow for the Center for Montessori Studies at UH and is a contributor to national research as an officer for URBAN CT.

**Kathleen Knight** (she/ella) is the Capacity Building Manager at The Fund for Santa Barbara, where she works with community to advance progressive change by strengthening movements for Economic, Environmental, Political, Racial, and Social Justice. Her work centers on co-creating experiential community education opportunities and facilitating deep relationship building. She facilitates the Central Coast Regional Equity Initiative, which advocates for social, health, environmental, and economic equity through region-wide cross-sector collaboration, community-led and research informed action, and an Indigenized and decolonized approach. A graduate of the University of California, Los Angeles, her field background is in tropical environmental science; she has engaged in research with jaguars in Costa Rica and worked on developing multi-stakeholder sustainable ebony management plans in the Congo Basin of Cameroon. She lived in and collaborated with the community of Guacimal, Costa Rica, while co-managing a community organizing center called el Centro Demostrativo de Sostenibilidad and working on various social justice projects.

**Paul Kuttner, EdD,** is a researcher, educator, and community engagement professional living in the Boston area. Paul is Director of Partnerships with Community-Campus Partnerships for Health (CCPH), a national nonprofit dedicated to health equity and social justice through partnerships between communities and academic institutions. In this role, Paul supports a large portfolio of community-engaged research and public health partnerships. Prior to joining CCPH, Paul served as Associate Director of University Neighborhood Partners (UNP) at the University of Utah, and as an instructor at the College of Education. Paul earned his master's and doctorate from the Harvard Graduate School of Education. His research focuses on the relationships between educational institutions (K-12 and higher education) and communities facing historical marginalization. His and his partners' research products have appeared in academic venues such as the *Journal of Higher Education Outreach and Engagement, Metropolitan Universities, Teachers College Record,* and *Harvard Educational Review,* as well as practice-focused outlets such as *Phi Delta Kappan* and *Ed Week,* alongside community-facing products such as videos, comic books, and curricula. Paul was named the 2023 Coalition of Urban and Metropolitan Universities (CUMU) Collaboratory Research Fellow for his work on evaluating the impact of community-campus partnerships.

**Zenia Lakhani,** a recent graduate from UC Berkeley, holds a Bachelor of Science in Molecular Environmental Biology, complemented by a minor in Public Policy. Guided by her passion for equity in healthcare, Zenia envisions a future where she can integrate medicine, policy, and public health to drive positive change. Zenia believes we must advocate for infrastructure-altering policy change that directly addresses the determinants of health, such as genetics, the environment, and access to quality healthcare.

**May Lin** (she/her) is an Assistant Professor of Asian & Asian American Studies at Cal State Long Beach. She is a community-rooted researcher & educator who supports transformative, intersectional, and cross-racial change led by communities of color, including stints as a Research Fellow/consultant for several youth & movement building organizing groups, including Californians for Justice and Youth Organize! California. She has been involved in Long Beach's racial justice organizing ecosystem since 2014, and is currently a board member of Khmer Girls in Action, Long Beach Forward, and a member of Long Beach People's Budget coalition. She draws upon previous organizing experience in youth development, grassroots media, graduate student unionizing, and grassroots organizing resisting gentrification. She has published on topics such as healing justice, co-governance and anti-racist futures in planning, and development of Asian American political consciousness in journals including *Health Affairs, Journal of the American Planning Association,* and *Journal of Ethnic & Migration Studies.* She is currently working on a collaborative multimedia project and manuscript to uplift Long Beach's healing justice and abolitionist movements.

**Morgan Love** (Tlingit) (she/her) is a Tlingit Native and Research Strategist at Evolve Equity Psychology, Inc. where her dedication lies in the integration of Indigenous methodologies throughout her research and evaluation practices. Holding a Bachelor's degree in Psychology with a minor in Global Health from the University of California, Los Angeles, Morgan is now a Master's candidate at the University College London studying Global Health and Development. With a specialized focus on community-led research and program evaluation through an Indigenous lens, Morgan employs advanced data analysis techniques to drive meaningful change within communities. Her mission is to reshape conventional Western research paradigms into comprehensive and holistic bodies of work that empower communities. She achieves this by equipping individuals and organizations with tools, training, and opportunities for capacity building in addition to strategic action planning and equity framework development. Noteworthy publications by Morgan include "American Indian and Alaska Native Substance Use Treatment: Barriers and Facilitators According to an Implementation Framework" (2023) and "Central Coast Regional Equity Initiative: Co-Creating and Actionizing a New Community-Led Equity Framework" (2023).

**Jarred Martinez** (he/him/el) was born and raised in Kearns, Utah, a grandchild of migrant workers who followed the fields, lover of cumbia, multidisciplinary creative, youth worker and father of a five-year old. As a community educator and partnership manager with University Neighborhood Partners, he works with youth, educators, and other allies to cultivate humanizing spaces where young people can develop critical literacy to practice transforming the world around them. Jarred's energy and passion are shaped by the work of remembering who and where we come from, unlearning colonized ways, and re-imagining a world where taking care of each other matters first.

**Elizabeth Montoya** The Community building is not just the core of Elizabeth's work, it is the core of who she is. Most days you can find Elizabeth in the Community Learning Center garden or kitchen, or delivering goods or food to neighbors on her big blue tricycle. Growing up in El Salvador, Elizabeth learned many things, from farming to cooking to the importance of love and support. Her work connects Glendale neighbors to each other and to the Salt Lake City school district.

**Alexis Mullard** With a Bachelor of Arts in Interdisciplinary Studies from UC Berkeley, specializing in Sustainable Design, Circular Fashion, Entrepreneurship, Business, and Technology, Alexis Mullard is dedicated to creating a more sustainable fashion industry. Alexis is a passionate advocate for sustainable fashion and social justice, which led her to found CINC COLLECTIVE, LLC, a circular and sustainable fashion brand. She is dedicated to making sustainable clothing and education on circular fashion accessible, while simultaneously encouraging other brands to alter their business models to incorporate sustainability and prioritize fair labor practices. Recently, Alexis has taken on the role of Production and Development Coordinator at a fashion brand, where she supports the brand's development and production standards by coordinating with the Director of Production, Product Development, and the Production Manager. Alexis manages a range of responsibilities from assisting the VP of Design, managing RLM data and shipping related to production, visiting factories, sourcing materials, managing photoshoot samples, and liaising with warehouses to managing the in-house Atelier, ensuring seamless integration between design, development, and production processes.

**Gilberto Rejon Magana** Gilberto, more commonly known as Coach Juan, is the founder of Hartland Community 4 Youth and Families. He has been a community advocate for more than 25 years and is committed to lifting up student and parent voices and creating pathways to higher education. Gilberto's perpetual grin and commitment to teaching and learning is a true community asset.

**Keri Taddie** As the coordinator of the Glendale-Mtn View Community Learning Center, Keri has dedicated 28 years to supporting the students, families, and staff. The relationships and programming she has built have been vital to the success of the Community Learning Center, where students, parents, and teachers can feel at home. In a place where more than 30 different languages are spoken, Keri builds a safe and empowering place to support education and community. Among numerous awards, Keri has recently earned Voices for Utah Children's *Hero in the Trenches Award* from for her amazing work strengthening student and parent success.

**Taylor Valci** (they/them) is a History major and Public Policy minor at UC Berkeley, specializing in 20th century American evangelicalism and labor practices, who chose to complete their bachelor's degree after working for several years as a Case Manager in the unhoused services sector. As an academic and activist, they are fiercely dedicated to developing scholarship surrounding the history and future dismantling of capitalism and white supremacy in both the evangelical industrial complex and the greater American labor system.

**Marcos Vargas** (Chicano Sundancer in the Lakota Tradition) is the Executive Director of the Fund for Santa Barbara. Prior to this, he served for 14 years as the founding Executive Director of CAUSE, a social justice organization serving the California Central Coast. Marcos' nonprofit experience also includes serving as the Executive Director of El Concilio del Condado de Ventura, a Latinx community advocacy and multi-service organization, and the Director of Planning for the United Way of Ventura County. He currently serves on several nonprofit boards, including the McCune Foundation, Runners for Public Lands, and Future Leaders of America. Awards have including the Outstanding Citizen Award from the California Federation of Teachers, Cesar Chavez Leadership Award from the United Farm Workers, Earth Summit Leadership Award from the Ventura County Citizens for Peaceful Resolution, and Leadership Award from the National Women's Political Caucus of Ventura County. Marcos has a doctorate and master's degree in urban planning from the UCLA. His dissertation addresses the expanding public policy and community development role of community-based organizations of color in California. He is a father of three children, an ultra-trail runner, agent of progressive social change, and Chicano Sundancer in the Lakota tradition. A strong advocate for indigenous peoples rights, Marcos sees Native ceremony, such as the traditional inipi sweat lodge purification ceremony and trail running as his medicine for bringing balance to his life, and connecting to the land, the creator, and the spirit of the land's first people.

**Jonnie Williams, PsyD** (Tódich'ii'nii Clan, Diné Nation), is a licensed clinical psychologist (CA, HI, NM), credentialed health service psychologist, prevention researcher, evaluator, and curriculum designer. Dr. Williams is the Founder and CEO of Evolve Equity Psychology, Inc. The vision of Evolve Equity is to advance health equity, racial justice, and systems change through indigenous worldview and scientific practices for groups that have been historically, socially, and economically marginalized. Evolve Equity provides research, evaluation, and training services to government agencies, corporations, philanthropic organizations, tribal nations, and nonprofits. Dr. Williams received her doctorate in Clinical Psychology in 2016 from an American Psychological Association-accredited program, the Wright Institute. As an integrated health, trauma, and pediatric psychologist, Dr.

Williams specializes in the evidence-based treatment of trauma-related disorders using culturally informed bio-psycho-social, cognitive-behavioral, and socio-ecological healing approaches. Publications include "Adverse Childhood Events and Adult Substance Abuse Among Urban and Reservation American Indians" (2016) and "Central Coast Regional Equity Initiative: Co-Creating and Actionizing a New Community-Led Equity Framework" (2023). In December 2021, she was honored as a recipient of the prestigious "Native American 40 Under 40" award by the National Center for American Indian Enterprise Development. She serves as a site visit psychologist for the American Academy of Pediatrics Committee on Native American Child Health and is a National Advisory Board Member for the Early Childhood Developmental Health Systems Evidence to Impact Center.

**Blanca Yagüe** is a PhD Candidate in Anthropology at the University of Utah. She has a Bachelor's in Environmental Science from the University of Granada, and a Master's in Amazonian Studies from the National University of Colombia, Sede Amazonia. Her dissertation research investigates Indigenous peoples' food systems and cultures in urban contexts in the Colombian Amazon, where she has been working for 15 years. She is also involved with collaborative food justice and food sovereignty projects in Salt Lake City, where she contributed to launching the SPARC Environmental Justice Lab at the University of Utah, and where she takes part in some grassroots movements and actions. Blanca's research is interdisciplinary, with a strong applied focus, and she has a preference for participatory and collaborative approaches. Additionally, she is involved with the University of Utah Prison Education Project. She enjoys trying new foods, especially if they include insects. She also likes swimming in cold waters, reading, quiet places, and siestas.

## INDEX

**T**



**U**



**W**